CAMBRIDGE LIBRARY COLLECTION

Books of enduring scholarly value

Literary Studies

This series provides a high-quality selection of early printings of literary works, textual editions, anthologies and literary criticism which are of lasting scholarly interest. Ranging from Old English to Shakespeare to early twentieth-century work from around the world, these books offer a valuable resource for scholars in reception history, textual editing, and literary studies.

George Smith – A Memoir

This 1902 book, originally intended for private circulation, is a memoir of George Smith (1824–1901), founder, proprietor and publisher of *The Cornhill Magazine* and later the *Dictionary of National Biography*. The small volume, compiled by Smith's wife, consists of a memoir of Smith by Sidney Lee, followed by four short autobiographical pieces that Smith wrote for *The Cornhill*. He recalls his years at the publishing house of Smith, Elder and Co.; his encounters with Charlotte Brontë, who stayed with the Smiths in London; his idea of founding a magazine; and the 'lawful pleasures' of court cases for libel. The final item is Sir Leslie Stephen's obituary of Smith, first published in *The Cornhill*. The book, illustrated with two portraits of Smith, and a photograph of his memorial tablet in St Paul's Cathedral, provides an engaging portrait of a significant Victorian publisher and man of letters.

T0345346

Cambridge University Press has long been a pioneer in the reissuing of out-of-print titles from its own backlist, producing digital reprints of books that are still sought after by scholars and students but could not be reprinted economically using traditional technology. The Cambridge Library Collection extends this activity to a wider range of books which are still of importance to researchers and professionals, either for the source material they contain, or as landmarks in the history of their academic discipline.

Drawing from the world-renowned collections in the Cambridge University Library and other partner libraries, and guided by the advice of experts in each subject area, Cambridge University Press is using state-of-the-art scanning machines in its own Printing House to capture the content of each book selected for inclusion. The files are processed to give a consistently clear, crisp image, and the books finished to the high quality standard for which the Press is recognised around the world. The latest print-on-demand technology ensures that the books will remain available indefinitely, and that orders for single or multiple copies can quickly be supplied.

The Cambridge Library Collection brings back to life books of enduring scholarly value (including out-of-copyright works originally issued by other publishers) across a wide range of disciplines in the humanities and social sciences and in science and technology.

George Smith
A Memoir

SIDNEY LEE
GEORGE SMITH
LESLIE STEPHEN

CAMBRIDGE
UNIVERSITY PRESS

CAMBRIDGE UNIVERSITY PRESS

Cambridge, New York, Melbourne, Madrid, Cape Town,
Singapore, São Paolo, Delhi, Mexico City

Published in the United States of America by Cambridge University Press, New York

www.cambridge.org
Information on this title: www.cambridge.org/9781108047647

© in this compilation Cambridge University Press 2012

This edition first published 1902
This digitally printed version 2012

ISBN 978-1-108-04764-7 Paperback

GEORGE SMITH

Walker & Cockerell, ph. sc

Yours sincerely
Smith

From the picture painted by G. F. Watts, R.A. in 1876.

GEORGE SMITH

A MEMOIR

WITH SOME PAGES OF AUTOBIOGRAPHY

FOR PRIVATE CIRCULATION

LONDON
1902

In this small volume I have brought together, for private circulation among my husband's friends, the four papers of Reminiscences which he contributed to the 'Cornhill Magazine' during the last months of his life, together with the In Memoriam notice from Sir Leslie Stephen's pen which appeared in the Magazine immediately after his death, and the fuller Memoir which Mr. Sidney Lee wrote for the first volume of the Supplement to the 'Dictionary of National Biography.'

I have also included reproductions of the two portraits of my husband : one painted of him in middle life, by Mr. G. F. Watts, R.A., and the other, a posthumous portrait by the Hon. John Collier, representing him in his latest years, which I owe to the kindness of the friends who desire that it should remain with me until offered to the National Portrait Gallery.

The friends of my dear husband have in many ways shown the affection and esteem in which they hold his memory, and I believe I am not wrong in thinking that they will welcome this small memorial of his career, which I beg them to accept with my grateful acknowledgments of their kindness and sympathy.

I am also glad to have this opportunity of expressing the deep gratification which the Memorial Tablet his friends have placed in St. Paul's Cathedral has given to me and to my children.

E. S.

August 1902.

CONTENTS

PAGE

A MEMOIR OF GEORGE SMITH BY SIDNEY LEE . . 1
*From the Supplement to the 'Dictionary of National
Biography.'*

SOME PAGES OF AUTOBIOGRAPHY BY GEORGE SMITH
From the 'Cornhill Magazine.'

   I. IN THE EARLY FORTIES 71

   II. CHARLOTTE BRONTË 82

   III. OUR BIRTH AND PARENTAGE 106

   IV. LAWFUL PLEASURES 126

IN MEMORIAM, BY SIR LESLIE STEPHEN, K.C.B. . . 147
From the 'Cornhill Magazine.'

PORTRAIT . . . . *Frontispiece*
*From the picture painted by Mr. G. F. Watts, R.A.,
in 1876.*

PORTRAIT . . . . *To face p.* 71
*From the posthumous picture painted by the Hon.
John Collier in 1901.*

MEMORIAL TABLET . . . . . . ,, 147

A MEMOIR

OF

GEORGE SMITH

Reprinted from the
Supplement to the 'Dictionary of National Biography'

B

MEMOIR OF GEORGE SMITH

I

GEORGE SMITH (1824–1901), publisher, the founder and proprietor of the 'Dictionary of National Biography,' was of Scottish parentage. His paternal grandfather was a small landowner and farmer in Morayshire (or Elginshire), who died young and left his family ill provided for. His father, George Smith (1789–1846), began life as an apprentice to Isaac Forsyth, a bookseller and banker in the town of Elgin. At a youthful age he migrated to London with no resources at his command beyond his abilities and powers of work. By nature industrious, conscientious, and religious, he was soon making steady and satisfactory progress. At first he found employment in the publishing house of Rivington in St. Paul's Churchyard. Subsequently he transferred his services to John Murray, the famous publisher of Albemarle Street, and while in Murray's employ was sent on one occasion to deliver proof-sheets to Lord Byron. At length, in 1816, he and another Scottish immigrant to London, Alexander Elder, a native of Banff, who was Smith's junior by a year, went into partnership, and set up in business for themselves on a modest scale. They opened premises at 158 Fenchurch Street as booksellers and stationers. The new firm was styled Smith & Elder. After three years the partners added publishing to the other branches of their business. On March 2, 1819, they were both admitted by redemption to the freedom of the Stationers' Company. Membership of the company was needful at the time for the pursuit in London of the publisher's calling. Some four months later, on July 19, 1819, Smith & Elder entered their earliest publication in the Stationers' Company's register. It was a well-printed collection of ' Sermons and Expositions of interesting Portions of Scripture,' by a popular congregational minister, Dr. John Morison of Trevor Chapel, Brompton. Thus unobtrusively did the publishing house set out on its road to fame and fortune, which it soon attained in moderate measure by dint of strenuous endeavour and skilful adaptation of means to ends.

On October 12, 1820—little more than a year after the elder Smith had become a London publisher—he married. His wife, Elizabeth Murray, then twenty-three years old, and thus her husband's junior by eight years, was daughter of Alexander Murray, a successful glass-ware manufacturer in London, who, like her husband, was of Elginshire origin. Mrs. Smith was a woman of much shrewdness, vivacity, and sanguine temper, in whose judgment and resourcefulness her husband, and afterwards her children, placed the utmost confidence. The young couple lived, on their marriage, over Smith & Elder's shop in Fenchurch Street, and there George Smith, the eldest son and second child (of six), was born on March 19, 1824.[1]

Very shortly after his birth the father removed his business and his family to 65 Cornhill—to that house which was fated to acquire wide repute, alike in literary and commercial circles. There, at the age of six, young George Smith suffered an attack of brain fever, and his mother, who showed him special indulgence, was warned

During the last twenty-eight years of his life Smith designated himself George M. Smith. He had bestowed his mother's name of Murray on all his children, and it was convenient to give a corresponding form to his own signature.

against subjecting him to any severity of discipline. From infancy he was active and high-spirited, and domestic leniency encouraged in him an unruliness of temper which hampered the course of his education. But his parents desired him to enjoy every educational advantage that lay in their power. At first he was sent to Dr. Smith's boarding school at Rottingdean. Thence he passed at the age of ten to Merchant Taylors' School, but soon left it for a school at Blackheath, where the master, finding him intractable, advised his parents, greatly to their indignation, to send him to sea. Although he did well as far as the schoolwork was concerned, his propensity for mischievous frolic was irrepressible, and after he had spent a few terms at the City of London School his father deemed it wisest to take him into his office. He had shown an aptitude for mathematics, delighted in chemistry, and had not neglected Latin ; but he was too young to have made great advance in the conventional subjects of study when in 1838, at the age of fourteen, he began a business career. Subsequently he received lessons at home in French, and showed a quick intuitive appreciation of good literature. But it was the stir of the mercantile world that first gave useful direction to his abundant mental energy.

During his boyhood his father's firm had made notable progress. On its removal to Cornhill, in 1824, Smith & Elder were joined by a third partner, and the firm assumed the permanent designation of Smith, Elder, & Co. The new partner was a man of brilliant and attractive gifts, if of weak and self-indulgent temperament. His entry into the concern greatly extended its sphere of action. His guardian, Æneas Macintosh, was chief partner in a great firm of Calcutta merchants, and this connection with India brought to the bookselling and publishing branches of Smith, Elder, & Co.'s business the new department of an Indian agency, which in course of time far outdistanced in commercial importance the rest of their work. At the outset the Indian operations were confined to the export of stationery and books to officers in the East India Company's service ; but gradually all manner of commodities was dealt with, banking responsibilities were undertaken, and Smith, Elder, & Co. ultimately left most of the other Indian agencies in London far behind alike in the variety and extent of their transactions.

It was to the third partner, who had become a liveryman of the Clothworkers' Company on March 1, 1837, that Smith was apprenticed on beginning his business career. On May 2, 1838, the fact of his apprenticeship was duly entered in the Clothworkers' Company's records.

At the moment that Smith joined the firm it had entered into close relations with Lieutenant Waghorn, the originator of the overland route to India. While Waghorn was experimenting with his new means of communicating with the east, Smith, Elder, & Co. acted as his agents, and published from 1837 the many pamphlets in which he pressed his schemes and opinions on public notice. Some of Smith's earliest reminiscences related to Waghorn's strenuous efforts to perfect his system, with which the boy's native activity of mind enabled him to sympathise very thoroughly. All the letters that were sent to India under Waghorn's supervision across the Isthmus of Suez and through the Red Sea were despatched from Smith, Elder, & Co.'s office in Cornhill, and those reaching England from India by the same route were delivered there on arriving in London. Young Smith willingly helped his seniors to ' play at post office,' and found that part of his duties thoroughly congenial. But as a whole his labours in Cornhill were arduous. He was at work from half-past seven in the morning till eight o'clock in the evening, with very short intervals. His father wisely trained him in all the practical details of the stationery and bookselling business. He had to mend the office quills, and was taught how to bind books and even compose type. The dinner-hour in the middle of the day he often, however, contrived to spend at Dyer's riding school in Finsbury Square, where he became an expert horseman. Riding remained all his life his main recreation. In 1841, three years after his entry into the firm, his family removed to Denmark Hill.

The steady increase in the firm's general business was accompanied by marked activity in the publishing department, and early in the thirties that department won an assured reputation. For the first development of the publishing branch Mr. Elder was largely responsible, and though he applied himself to it somewhat spasmodically, and his ventures were by no means uniformly successful, some interesting results were quickly achieved. As early as 1826 Smith, Elder, & Co. issued, in partnership with Chalmers & Collins, a Glasgow firm, James Donnegan's 'New Greek and English Lexicon,' which was long a standard book. In 1827 they undertook single-handed the issue of Richard Thomson's 'Chronicles of London Bridge.' Of more popular literary work which the firm produced, the most attractive item was the fashionable annual called 'Friendship's Offering.' This elaborately illustrated gift-book was originally produced at the end of 1824, under the editorship of Thomas Kibble Hervey (subsequently editor of the 'Athenæum'), by a neighbouring publisher, Lupton Relfe of 13 Cornhill. The number for 1828 was the first published by Smith, Elder, & Co., and for fourteen consecutive years they continued to make annually an addition to the series. Hervey was succeeded in the editorship by the Scottish poet, Thomas Pringle, and ultimately by Leitch Ritchie, a well-known figure in journalism, who otherwise proved of service to the firm. The writers in 'Friendship's Offering' were the most distinguished of the day. They included not only veterans like Southey, Coleridge, and the Ettrick Shepherd, but also beginners like Tennyson and Ruskin.

The Hon. Mrs. Norton, Miss Mitford, Miss Strickland, were regular contributors. To the volume for 1833 Macaulay contributed his ' Ballad of the Armada.' The numerous plates in each issue were after pictures by the greatest artists of the time, and were engraved by the best available talent. When the series was at its zenith of popularity some eight to ten thousand copies of each volume were sold at Christmas.

Another of the literary connections of the firm was Miss Louisa Henrietta Sheridan, a daughter of Captain W. B. Sheridan, a very distant relative of the well-known family.[1] Of her personal attractions Smith cherished from boyhood admiring memories. Between 1831 and 1835 she edited for the firm five annual volumes entitled ' The Comic Offering, or Lady's Mélange of Literary Mirth,' which Robert Seymour, the practical originator of ' Pickwick,' helped to illustrate; and in 1838 Smith, Elder, & Co. produced for her ' The Diadem, a Book for the Boudoir,' with some valuable plates, and contributions by various well-known hands, including Thomas Campbell, James and Horace Smith, and Agnes Strickland.

In its attitude to fiction the young firm manifested, under Leitch Ritchie's influence, an exceptional spirit of enterprise. In 1833 Smith, Elder, & Co. started a ' Library of Romance,' a series of original novels and romances, English, American, or translated from foreign tongues, which they published at the prophetic price of six shillings. Fifteen volumes appeared under Ritchie's editorship before the series ended in 1835. The first was ' The Ghost Hunter and his Family,' by John and Michael Banim, the authors of ' The O'Hara Family ; ' the fourth was John Galt's ' Stolen Child ' (1833) ; the sixth, ' The Slave-King,' a translation from Victor Hugo (1833) ; and the fifteenth and last was ' Ernesto,' a philosophical

---

On Sept. 8, 1840, she married at Paris Lieut.-colonel Sir Henry Wyatt and died next year, Oct. 2, 1841.

romance of interest by William [Henry] Smith (1808–1872), who afterwards won fame as author of 'Thorndale.' Among Smith, Elder, & Co.'s early works in general light literature which still retain their zest were James Grant's 'Random Recollections of the House of Commons' and 'Random Recollections of the House of Lords' (1836). Nor was the firm disinclined to venture on art publications involving somewhat large risks. Clarkson Stanfield's 'Coast Scenery,' a collection of forty views, issued (after publication in serial parts) at the price of 32s. 6d., appeared in 1836; and 'The Byron Gallery,' thirty-six engravings of subjects from Byron's poems, followed soon afterwards at the price of 35s. These volumes met with a somewhat cool reception from the book-buying public, but an ambition to excel in the production of expensively illustrated volumes was well alive in the firm when, in 1838, Smith first enlisted in its service.[1] That year saw the issue of the first portion of the great collected edition of Sir Humphry Davy's 'Works,' which was completed in nine volumes next year. In 1838, too, the firm inaugurated a series of elaborate reports of recent expeditions which the government had sent out for purposes of scientific exploration. The earliest of these great scientific publications was Sir Andrew Smith's 'Illustrations of the Zoology of South Africa,' of which the first volume was issued in 1838, and four others followed between that date and 1847, all embellished with drawings of exceptional beauty by George Henry Ford. The government made a grant of 1,500l. in aid of the publication, and the five volumes were sold at the high price of 18l. Of like character were

---

[1] Besides the large ventures which they undertook on their own account, Smith, Elder, & Co. acted at this time as agents for many elaborate publications prepared by responsible publishers of Edinburgh and Glasgow; such were Thomas Brown's *Fossil Conchology of Great Britain*, the first of the twenty-eight serial parts of which appeared in April 1837, and Kay's *Edinburgh Portraits*, 2 vols. 4to. 1838.

the reports of the scientific results of Admiral Sir Edward
Belcher's voyage to the Pacific in the Sulphur : a volume
on the zoology, prepared by Richard Brinsley Hinds, came
out under Smith, Elder, & Co.'s auspices in 1843, a second
volume (on the botany) appeared in the next year, and a
third volume (completing the zoology) in 1845. That
was Smith, Elder, & Co.'s third endeavour in this special
class of publication. To the second a more lasting interest
attaches. It was ' The Zoological Report of the Expedition of H.M.S. Beagle,' in which Darwin sailed as naturalist. One thousand pounds was advanced by the government to the firm for the publication of this important
work. The first volume appeared in large quarto in 1840.
Four more volumes completed the undertaking by 1848,
the price of the whole being 8l. 15s. Smith, Elder, & Co.
were thus brought into personal relations with Darwin,
the earliest of their authors who acquired worldwide fame.
Independently of his official reports they published for
him, in more popular form, extracts from them in volumes
bearing the titles ' The Structure and Distribution of Coral
Reefs' in 1842, ' Geological Observations on Volcanic
Islands' in 1844, and ' Geological Observations on South
America ' in 1846.

The widening range of the firm's dealings with distant
lands in its capacity of Indian agents rendered records of
travel peculiarly appropriate to its publishing department,
and Smith, Elder, & Co. boldly contemplated the equip-
ment on their own account of explorers whose reports
should serve them as literature. About 1840 Austen
Henry Layard set out, at their suggestion, in the company
of Edward Mitford, on an overland journey to Asia ; but
the two men quarrelled on the road, and the work that
the firm contemplated was never written. Another
project which was defeated by a like cause was an
expedition to the south of France, on which Leitch Ritchie
and James Augustus St. John started in behalf of Smith,
Elder, & Co.'s publishing department. But the firm was

never dependent on any single class of publication. It is noteworthy that no sooner had it opened relations with Darwin, the writer who was to prove the greatest English naturalist of the century, than its services were sought by him who was to prove the century's greatest art-critic and one of its greatest artists in English prose—John Ruskin. It was in 1843, while Smith was still in his pupilage, that Ruskin's father, a prosperous wine merchant in the city of London, introduced his son's first prose work to Smith, Elder, & Co.'s notice. They had already published some poems by the young man in 'Friendship's Offering.' In 1843 he had completed the first volume of 'Modern Painters, by a Graduate of Oxford.' His father failed to induce John Murray to issue it on commission. The offer was repeated at Cornhill, where it was accepted with alacrity, and thus was inaugurated Ruskin's thirty years' close personal connection with Smith, Elder, & Co., and more especially with George Smith, on whose shoulders the whole responsibilities of the firm were soon to fall.

The public were slow in showing their appreciation of Ruskin's earliest book. Of the five hundred copies printed of the first edition of the first volume of ' Modern Painters,' only 105 were disposed of within the year. Possibly there were other causes besides public indifference for this comparative failure. Signs were not wanting at the moment that, ambitious and enlightened as were many of the young firm's publishing enterprises, they suffered in practical realisation from a lack of strict business method which it was needful to supply, if the publishing department was to achieve absolute success. The heads of the firm were too busily absorbed in their rapidly growing Indian business to give close attention to the publishing branch ; managers had been recently chosen to direct it, and had not proved sufficiently competent to hold their posts long. Salvation was at hand within the office from a quarter in which the partners had not thought to seek it. A predilection for the publishing branch of the business was already declaring itself in young Smith, as well as a practical insight into business method which convinced him, boy though he was, that some reorganisation was desirable. With a youthful self-confidence, which, contrary to common experience, events showed to be justifiable, he persuaded his father late in 1843—a few months after the issue of the first volume of 'Modern Painters,' and when he was in his twentieth year—to allow him to assume, temporarily at any rate, control of the publishing department. Under cautious conditions his father acceded to his wish, and Smith at once accepted for publication a collection of essays by various writers on well-known literary people, edited by the somewhat eccentric and impracticable author of 'Orion,' Richard Hengist Horne. The enterprise called forth all Smith's energies. Not only did he supervise the production of the work, which was adorned by eight steel engravings, but, in constant interviews with the author, he freely urged alterations in the text which he deemed needful to conciliate public taste. The book appeared, in February 1844, in two volumes, with the title 'The New Spirit of the Age,' and Smith had the satisfaction of securing for his firm fair pecuniary profit from this his earliest publication. Another edition was reached in July. His second publishing venture was from the pen of a somewhat miscellaneous practitioner in literature, Mrs. Baron Wilson, who had contributed to Miss Sheridan's 'Diadem' as well as to 'Friendship's Offering.' For her he published, also in 1844 (in June), another work in two volumes, 'Our Actresses, or Glances at Stage Favourites Past and Present,' with five engravings in each volume, including portraits of Miss O'Neill, Miss Helen Faucit, and Mrs. Charles Kean. His third literary undertaking in the first year of his publishing career was of more permanent interest ; it was Leigh Hunt's 'Imagination and Fancy.' It was characteristic of Smith's whole life as a publisher that he was never content to maintain with authors merely formal business relations. From boyhood the personality of writers of repute deeply interested him, and that interest never diminished at any point of his career. In early manhood he was rarely happier than in the society of authors of all degrees of ability. With a city clerk of literary leanings, Thomas Powell,[1] he was as a youth on friendly terms, and at Powell's house at Peckham he was first introduced to, or came to hear of, many rising men of letters. It was there that he first met Horne, and afterwards Robert Browning. It was there that he found the manuscript of Leigh Hunt's ' Imagination and Fancy,' and at once visited the author in Edwardes Square, Kensington, with a generous offer for the rights of publication which was immediately accepted. Thenceforth Leigh Hunt was a valued literary acquaintance, and Smith published for him a whole library of attractive essays or compilations. Another house at which he was a frequent guest at this early period was that of Ruskin's father at Denmark Hill. Powell introduced him to a small convivial club, called the Museum Club, which met in a street off the Strand. Douglas Jerrold and Father Prout were prominent members. There he first made the acquaintance of George Henry Lewes, who became a lifelong associate. The club, however, fell into pecuniary difficulties, from which Smith strove in vain to relieve it, and it quickly dissolved.

The grim realities of life were soon temporarily to restrict Smith's opportunities of recreation. Towards the end of 1844 a grave calamity befell his family. His father's health failed ; softening of the brain declared itself ; and recovery was seen to be hopeless. The elder

---

[1] In 1849 Powell emigrated to America, where he became a professional man of letters, and published some frankly ill-natured sketches of writers he had met, under the title of *Living Authors of England* ; this was followed by *Living Authors of America* (first series, 1850).

Smith removed from Denmark Hill to Boxhill, where he acquired some eight to ten acres of land, and developed a lively interest in farming. But he was unable to attend to the work of the firm, and his place at Cornhill was taken by his son very soon after he came of age in 1845. On May 3, 1846, George Smith was admitted by patrimony a freeman of the Stationers' Company, and little more than three months later his father died, at the age of fifty-seven (Aug. 21, 1846). Thereupon the whole responsibility of providing for his mother, his young brothers and sisters, devolved upon him.

II

Smith had no sooner addressed himself to his heavy task than he found himself face to face with a crisis in the affairs of the firm of exceptional difficulty for so young a man to grapple with. The third partner was discovered to be misusing the firm's credit and capital, and had to withdraw from the partnership under circumstances that involved grave anxiety to all concerned.[1] Elder, who had not of late years given close attention to the business, made up his mind to retire almost at the same time.[2] Smith was thus left to conduct single-handed the firm's affairs at a moment when the utmost caution and financial skill were required to maintain its equilibrium. Although no more than twenty-two, he proved himself equal to the situation. By a rare combination of sagacity and daring, by a masterful yet tactful exercise of authority, and by unremitting application, he was able to set the firm's affairs in order, to unravel the complications due to neglected bookkeeping, and to launch the concern anew on a career of prosperity far greater than that it had previously known.

[1] He went to India and died at Calcutta, Jan. 13, 1852.
[2] Mr. Elder left London and died some thirty years later, on Feb. 6, 1876, at Lancing, at the age of eighty-six.

For a time the major part of his energies and business instinct was devoted to the control and extension of the agency and banking department. It is difficult to over-estimate the powers of work which he brought to his task. ' It was a common thing for me,' he wrote of this period, ' and many of the clerks to work until three or four o'clock in the morning, and occasionally, when there was but a short interval between the arrival and departure of the Indian mails, I used to start work at nine o'clock of one morning, and neither leave my room nor cease dictating until seven o'clock the next evening, when the mail was despatched. During these thirty-two hours of continuous work I was supported by mutton chops and green tea at stated intervals. I believe I maintained my health by active exercise on foot and horseback, and by being able, after these excessive stretches of work, to sleep soundly for many hours ; on these occasions I generally got to bed at about eleven, and slept till three or four o'clock the next afternoon.' [1]

Astonishing success followed Smith's efforts. The profits rose steadily, and the volume of business, which was well under 50,000l. when he assumed control of the concern, multiplied thirteen times within twenty years of his becoming its moving spirit. The clerks at Cornhill in a few years numbered 150. An important branch was established at Bombay, and other agencies were opened at Java and on the West Coast of Africa. There was no manner of merchandise for which Smith's clients could apply to him in vain. Scientific instruments for surveying purposes, the testing of which needed the closest supervision, were regularly forwarded to the Indian government. The earliest electric telegraph plant that reached India was despatched from Cornhill. It was an ordinary experience to export munitions of war. On one occasion Smith was able to answer the challenge of a scoffer who thought to name an exceptional article of commerce—a human skeleton—which it would be beyond his power to supply, by displaying in his office two or three waiting to be packed for transit.

Smith's absorption in the intricate details of the firm's general operations prevented him from paying close attention to the minutiæ of the publishing department; but the fascination that it exerted on him never slept, and he wisely brought into the office one who was well qualified to give him literary counsel, and could be trusted to keep the department faithful to the best traditions of English publishing. His choice fell on William Smith Williams, who for nearly thirty years acted as his 'reader' or literary adviser. The circumstances under which he invited Williams's co-operation illustrate the accuracy with which he measured men and their qualifications. At the time the two met, Williams was clerk to Hullmandel & Walter, a firm of lithographers who were working for Smith, Elder, & Co. on Darwin's 'The Voyage of H.M.S. Beagle.' On assuming the control of the Cornhill business Smith examined with Williams the somewhat complicated accounts of that undertaking. After very brief intercourse he perceived that Williams was an incompetent bookkeeper, but had exceptional literary knowledge and judgment. No time was lost in inducing Williams to enter the service of Smith, Elder, & Co., and the arrangement proved highly beneficial and congenial to both.[1] But Smith

William Smith Williams (1800–1875) played a useful part behind the scenes of the theatre of nineteenth-century literature. He was by nature too modest to gain any wide recognition. He began active life in 1817 as apprentice to the publishing firm of Taylor & Hessey of Fleet Street, who published writings of Charles Lamb, Coleridge, and Keats, and became in 1821 proprietors of the *London Magazine*. Williams cherished from boyhood a genuine love of literature, and received much kindly notice from eminent writers associated with Taylor & Hessey. Besides Keats, he came to know Leigh Hunt and William Hazlitt. Marrying at twenty-five he opened a bookshop on his own account in a court near the Poultry, but delegated to none the master's responsibility in any branch of the business, and, though publishing negotiations were thenceforth often initiated by Williams, there were few that were not concluded personally by Smith.

For some time after he became sole owner and manager at Cornhill, Smith felt himself in no position to run large risks in the publishing department. A cautious policy was pursued ; but fortune proved kind. It was necessary to carry to completion those great works of scientific travel by Sir Andrew Smith, Hinds, and Darwin, the publication of which had been not only contracted for, but was actually in progress during Smith's pupilage. The firm had also undertaken the publication of a *magnum opus* of Sir John Herschel—his 'Astronomical Observations made at the Cape of Good Hope'—towards the expense of which the Duke of Northumberland had offered

insufficient capital compelled him to relinquish this venture in 1827, when he entered the counting-house of the lithographic printers, Hullmandel & Walter, where Smith met him. At that time he was devoting his leisure to articles on literary or theatrical topics for the *Spectator*, *Athenæum*, and other weekly papers. During the thirty years that he spent in Smith's employ he won, by his sympathetic criticism and kindly courtesy, the cordial regard of many distinguished authors whose works Smith, Elder, & Co. published. The paternal consideration that he showed to Charlotte Brontë is well known ; it is fully described in Mrs. Gaskell's *Life* of Miss Brontë.   He was my first favourable critic,' wrote Charlotte Brontë in December 1847 ; ' he first gave me encouragement to persevere as an author.' When she first saw him at Cornhill in 1848, she described him as ' a pale, mild, stooping man of fifty.' Subsequently she thought him too much given to ' contemplative theorising,' and possessed by ' too many abstractions.' With Thackeray, Ruskin, and Lewes he was always on very friendly terms. During his association with Smith he did no independent literary work beyond helping to prepare for the firm, in 1861, a *Selection from the Writings of John Ruskin*. He was from youth a warm admirer of Ruskin, sharing especially his enthusiasm for Turner. Williams retired from Smith, Elder, & Co.'s business in February 1875, and died six months later, aged 75, at his residence at Twickenham (August 21). His eldest daughter was the wife of Mr. Lowes Dickinson, the well-known portrait painter; and his youngest daughter, Miss Anna Williams, achieved distinction as a singer.

1,000*l.* The work duly appeared in 1846 in royal quarto, with eighteen plates, at the price of four guineas. A like obligation incurred by the firm in earlier days was fulfilled by the issue, also in 1846, of the naturalist Hugh Falconer's 'Fauna Antiqua Sivalensis.' Nine parts of this important work were issued at a guinea each in the course of the three years 1846–9. In 1846, too, Ruskin completed the second volume of his 'Modern Painters,' of which an edition of 1,500 copies was issued; and in 1849 Smith brought out the second of Ruskin's great prose works, 'The Seven Lamps of Architecture,' which was the earliest of Ruskin's books that was welcomed with practical warmth on its original publication.

In fiction the chief author with whom Smith in the first years of his reign at Cornhill was associated was the grandiloquent writer of blood-curdling romance, G. P. R. James. In 1844 Smith, Elder, & Co. had begun an elaborate collected edition of his works, of which they issued eleven volumes by 1847, ten more being undertaken by another firm. Unhappily Smith, Elder, & Co. had also independently entered into a contract with James to publish every new novel that he should write; 600*l.* was to be paid for the first edition of 1,250 copies. The arrangement lasted for four years, and then sank beneath its own weight. The firm issued two novels by James in each of the years 1845, 1846, 1847, and no less than three in 1848. Each work was in three volumes, at the customary price of 31*s.* 6*d.*; so that between 1845 and 1848 Smith offered the public twenty-seven volumes from James's pen at a total cost to the purchasers of thirteen and a half guineas. James's fertility was clearly greater than the public approved. The publisher requested him to set limits to his annual output. He indignantly declined, but Smith persisted with success in his objections to the novelist's interpretation of the original agreement, and author and publisher parted company. In 1848 Smith issued a novel by his friend, George Henry Lewes, entitled 'Rose, Blanche, and Violet.' Although much was expected from it, nothing came.

While the tragi-comedy of James was in its last stage, Smith became the hero of a publishing idyll which had the best possible effect on his reputation as a publisher and testified at the same time to his genuine kindness of heart Few episodes in the publishing history of the nineteenth century are of higher interest than the story of his association with Charlotte Brontë. In July 1847 Williams called Smith's attention to a manuscript novel entitled 'The Professor,' which had been sent to the firm by an author writing under the name of 'Currer Bell.' The manuscript showed signs of having vainly sought the favour of other publishing houses. Smith and his assistant recognised the promise of the work, but neither thought it likely to be a successful publication. While refusing it, however, they encouraged the writer in kindly and appreciative terms to submit another effort. The manuscript of 'Jane Eyre' arrived at Cornhill not long afterwards. Williams read it and handed it to Smith. The young publisher was at once fascinated by its surpassing power, and purchased the copyright out of hand. He always regarded the manuscript, which he retained, as the most valued of his literary treasures. He lost no time in printing it, and in 1848 the reading world recognised that he had introduced to its notice a novel of abiding fame. Later in 1848 'Shirley,' by 'Currer Bell,' was also sent to Cornhill. So far 'Currer Bell' had conducted the correspondence with the firm as if the writer were a man, but Smith shrewdly suspected that the name was a woman's pseudonym. His suspicions were confirmed in the summer of 1848, when Charlotte Brontë, accompanied by her sister Anne, presented herself without warning at Cornhill in order to explain some misunderstanding which she thought had arisen in the negotiations for the publication of 'Shirley.' From the date of the authoress's shy and unceremonious introduction of herself to him at his office desk until her premature death some seven years later, Smith's personal relations with her were characterised by a delightfully unaffected chivalry. On their first visit to Cornhill he took Miss Brontë and her sister to the opera the same evening. Smith's mother made their acquaintance next day, and they twice dined at her residence, then at 4 Westbourne Place. Miss Brontë frankly confided to a friend a day or two later her impressions of her publisher-host. 'He is a firm, intelligent man of business, though so young [he was only twenty-four]; bent on getting on, and I think desirous of making his way by fair, honourable means. He is enterprising, but likewise cool and cautious. Mr. Smith is a practical man.' [1]

On this occasion the sisters stayed in London only three days. But next year, in November 1849, Miss Brontë was the guest of Smith's mother at Westbourne Place for nearly three weeks. She visited the London sights under Smith's guidance; he asked Thackeray, whose personal acquaintance he does not seem to have made previously, to dine with him in order to satisfy her ambition of meeting the great novelist, whose work aroused in her the warmest enthusiasm. On returning to Haworth in December she wrote to Smith : 'Very easy is it to discover that with you to gratify others is to gratify yourself ; to serve others is to afford yourself a pleasure. I suppose you will experience your share of ingratitude and encroachments, but do not let them alter you. Happily they are the less likely to do this because you are half a Scotchman, and therefore must have inherited a fair share of prudence to qualify your generosity, and of caution to protect your benevolence.' [2]

---

[1] *Cornhill Magazine*, December 1900 ; cf. Gaskell's *Life*, ed. Shorter, p. 368 *n.*

[2] Gaskell's *Life*, ed. Shorter, p. 433.

Another visit—a fortnight long—followed in June 1850. Smith had then removed with his mother to 76 (afterwards 112) Gloucester Terrace. Miss Brontë renewed her acquaintance with Thackeray, who invited her and her host to dine at his own house, and she met Lewes under Smith's roof. Before she quitted London on this occasion she sat to George Richmond for her portrait at the instance of her host, who gratified her father by presenting him with the drawing together with an engraving of his and his daughter's especial hero, the Duke of Wellington. Next month, in July 1850, Smith made with a sister a tour in the Highlands of Scotland, and he always remembered with pride a friendly meeting that befell him on the journey with Macaulay, who was on his way to explore Glencoe and Killiecrankie. At Edinburgh he and his sister were joined on his invitation by Miss Brontë, and they devoted a few days to visiting together sites of interest in the city and its neighbourhood, much to Miss Brontë's satisfaction. She travelled south with them, parting from them in Yorkshire for her home at Haworth.[1] For a third time she was her sympathetic publisher's guest in London, in June 1851, when she stayed a month with his mother, and he took her to hear Thackeray's 'Lectures on the Humourists' at Willis's Rooms. In a letter addressed to Smith, on arriving home, she described him as 'the most spirited and vigilant of publishers.' In November 1852 Miss Brontë sent to the firm her manuscript of 'Villette,' in which she drew her portrait of Smith in the soundhearted, manly, and sensible Dr. John, while his mother was the original of Mrs. Bretton. In January 1853 Miss Brontë visited Smith and his family for the last time. They continued to correspond with each other till near her premature death on March 31, 1855.

An interesting result of Smith's personal and

---

[1] Mrs. Gaskell's *Life of Charlotte Brontë*, ed. Shorter, pp. 460 *sq.*

professional relations with Charlotte Brontë was to make him known to such writers as were her friends—notably to Harriet Martineau and to Mrs. Gaskell, for both of whom he subsequently published much. But more important is it to record that Charlotte Brontë was a main link in the chain that drew a writer of genius far greater even than her own—Thackeray himself—into Smith's history and into the history of his firm. In the late autumn of 1850, after the interchange of hospitalities which Miss Brontë's presence in London had prompted, Thackeray asked Smith for the first time to publish a book for him, his next Christmas book. It was a humorous sketch, with drawings by himself, entitled ' The Kickleburys on the Rhine.' Thackeray's regular publishers, Chapman & Hall, had not been successful with his recent Christmas books, ' Doctor Birch and his Young Friend ' and ' Rebecca and Rowena,' and they deprecated the issue of another that year. Smith had from early days, since he read the ' Paris Sketch-book ' by stealth in Tegg's sale rooms, cherished a genuine affection for Thackeray's work, and it had been a youthful ambition to publish for him. Williams had in his behalf made a vain bid for ' Vanity Fair ' in 1848. Smith now purchased the copyright of ' The Kickleburys ' with alacrity, and it was published at Christmas 1850 in an edition of three thousand. Though it was heavily bombarded by the ' Times,' it proved successful and at once reached a second edition.[1] In 1851, when Smith heard that Thackeray was engaged on a new work of importance—which proved to be 'Esmond'—he called at his house in Young Street, Kensington, and offered him what was then the handsome sum of 1,200l. for the right of issuing the first edition of 2,500 copies.[2]

---

[1] *The Kickleburys* bore on the title-page the actual year of publication, i.e. 1850. Thackeray's earlier and later Christmas books were each post-dated by a year. Thus *Rebecca and Rowena*, which bears the date 1850 was published in December 1849.

[2] Cf. Mrs. Ritchie's *Chapters from some Memoirs*, 1894, p. 130.

Thenceforth he was on close terms of intimacy with
Thackeray.   He was often at his house, and showed as
tender a consideration for the novelist's young daughters
as for Thackeray himself. ' Esmond ' appeared in 1852 and
was the first of Thackeray's novels to be published in the
regulation trio of half-a-guinea volumes.   Just before its
publication, when Thackeray was preparing to start on a
lecturing tour in America, Smith, with kindly thought,
commissioned Samuel Laurence to draw Thackeray's
portrait, so that his daughters might have a competent
presentment of him at home during his absence.   Before
Thackeray's return Smith published his ' Lectures on the
English Humourists,' and, in order to make the volume of
more presentable size, added elaborate notes by Thackeray's
friend James Hannay.   In December 1854 Smith published the best known of Thackeray's Christmas books,
' The Rose and the Ring.' [1]

III

Meanwhile Smith's private and business life alike
underwent important change.   The pressure of constant
application was, in 1853, telling on his health, and he resolved to share his responsibilities with a partner.   Henry
Samuel King, a bookseller of Brighton, whose bookselling
establishment is still carried on there by Treacher & Co.,
came to Cornhill to aid in the general superintendence
and to receive a quarter share of the profits.   His previous
experience naturally gave him a particular interest in the
publishing department.   On July 3, 1853, Charlotte Brontë
wrote to Smith : ' I hope your partner Mr. King will soon
acquire a working faculty and leave you some leisure and
opportunity effectually to cultivate health.'   At the same

[1] Thackeray was not yet, however, exclusively identified with Smith,
Elder, & Co. *The Newcomes* in 1853-5, a collected edition of Miscellaneous
Writings in 1855-7 (4 vols.), and *The Virginians*, 1857-9, were all issued
by Bradbury & Evans

date Smith became engaged to Elizabeth, the daughter of
John Blakeway, a wine merchant of London, and grand-
daughter of Edward Blakeway, esq., of Broseley Hall, Shrop-
shire. The marriage took place on February 11, 1854.
For four years he and his wife lived at 112 Gloucester
Terrace, where he had formerly resided with his mother.
Subsequently they spent some time at Wimbledon, and at
the end of 1859 they settled at 11 Gloucester Square.

Smith felt from the outset that the presence of a
partner at Cornhill hampered his independence, but it
relieved him of some labour and set him free to entertain
new developments of business. One of his early hopes
was to become proprietor of a newspaper, and during 1854
he listened with much interest to a suggestion made to him
by Thackeray that the novelist should edit a daily sheet of
general criticism after the manner of Addison and Steele's
'Spectator' or 'Tatler.' The sheet was to be called 'Fair
Play,' was to deal with literature as well as life, and was
to be scrupulously frank and just in comment. But, as
the discussion on the subject advanced, Thackeray feared
to face the responsibilities of editorship, and Smith was
left to develop the scheme for himself at a later period.
Newspapers of more utilitarian type were, however,
brought into being by him and his firm before the notion
of 'Fair Play' was quite dropped. In 1855 Smith, Elder,
& Co. started a weekly periodical called 'The Overland
Mail,' of which Mr. (afterwards Sir) John Kaye became
editor. It was to supply home information to readers in
India. Next year a complementary periodical was inaugurated under the title of 'The Homeward Mail,' which was
intended to offer Indian news to readers in the United
Kingdom. 'The Homeward Mail' was placed in the
charge of E. B. Eastwick, the Orientalist. The two editors
were already associated as authors with the firm. Both
papers were appreciated by the clients of the firm's agency
and banking departments, and are still in existence.

In order to facilitate the issue of these ' Mails ' Smith, Elder, & Co. acquired for the first time a printing office of their own. They took over premises in Little Green Arbour Court, Old Bailey, which had been occupied by Stewart & Murray, a firm of printers whose partners were relatives of Mr. Elder. The house had been the home of Goldsmith, and Smith was much interested in that association. Until 1872, when the printing office was made over to Messrs. Spottiswoode & Co., a portion of Smith, Elder, & Co.'s general literary work was printed at their own press.

In 1857 the progress of the firm received a temporary check. The outbreak of the Indian mutiny dislocated all Indian business, and Smith, Elder, and Co.'s foreign department suffered severely. Guns and ammunition were the commodities of which their clients in India then stood chiefly in need, and they were accordingly sent out in ample quantities. Jacob's Horse and Hodson's Horse were both largely equipped from Cornhill, and the clerks there had often little to do beyond oiling and packing revolvers. It was a time of grave anxiety for the head of the firm. The telegraph wires were constantly bringing him distressing news of the murder of the firm's clients, many of whom were personally known to him. The massacres in India also meant pecuniary loss. Accounts were left unpaid, and it was difficult to determine the precise extent of outstanding debts that would never be discharged. But Smith's sanguine and resourceful temper enabled him to weather the storm, and the crisis passed without permanent injury to his position. Probably more damaging to the immediate interests of Smith, Elder, & Co. was the transference of the government of India in 1858 from the old Company to the Crown. Many of the materials for public works which private firms had supplied to the old East India Company and their officers were now provided by the new India Office without the

intervention of agents ; and the operations of Smith, Elder,
& Co.'s Indian branch had to seek other channels than of old.

The publishing department invariably afforded Smith
a means of distraction from the pressure of business cares
elsewhere. Its speculative character, which his caution
and sagacity commonly kept within reasonable limits of
safety, appealed to one side of his nature, while the social
intimacies which the work of publishing fostered appealed
strongly to another side. The rapid strides made in
public favour by Ruskin, whose greatest works Smith
published between 1850 and 1860, were an unfailing source
of satisfaction. In 1850 he had produced Ruskin's
fanciful ' King of the Golden River.' Next year came the
first volume of ' Stones of Venice,' the pamphlets on ' The
Construction of Sheepfolds,' and ' Pre-Raphaelitism,' and
the portfolio of ' Examples of the Architecture of Venice.'
The two remaining volumes of ' Stones of Venice '
followed in 1853. In 1854 appeared ' Lectures on
Architecture and Painting,' with two pamphlets ; and
then began the ' Notes on the Royal Academy,' which
were continued each year till 1859. In 1856 came the
elaborately illustrated third and fourth volumes of
' Modern Painters ; ' in 1857, ' Elements of Drawing,'
' Political Economy of Art,' and ' Notes on Turner's
Pictures ; ' in 1858, an engraving by Holl of Richmond's
drawing of Ruskin ; in 1859, ' The Two Paths,' ' Elements
of Perspective,' and the ' Oxford Museum ; ' and in 1860,
the fifth and final volume of ' Modern Painters.' The
larger books did not have a rapid sale, but many of the
cheaper volumes and pamphlets sold briskly. It was at
Ruskin's expense, too, that Smith prepared for publication
the first volume that was written by Ruskin's friend,
Dante Gabriel Rossetti, ' The Early Italian Poets,' 1861.
In 1850 Ruskin's father proved the completeness of his
confidence in Smith by presenting him with one of the
few copies of the volume of his son's ' Poems ' which his

paternal pride had caused to be printed privately. Smith remained through this period a constant visitor at the Ruskins' house at Denmark Hill, and there he made the welcome addition to his social circle of a large number of artists. Of these Millais became the fastest of friends; while Leighton, John Leech, Richard Doyle, (Sir) Frederic Burton, and the sculptor Alexander Monro were always held by him in high esteem.

It was at Ruskin's house that Smith was introduced to Wilkie Collins, son of a well-known artist. He declined to publish Collins's first story, ' Antonina,' because the topic seemed too classical for general taste, and he neglected some years later to treat quite seriously Collins's offer of his 'Woman in White,' with the result that a profitable investment was missed ; but in 1856 he accepted the volume of short stories called 'After Dark,' and thus began business relations with Collins which lasted intermittently for nearly twenty years.

In the late fifties Charlotte Brontë's introduction of Smith to Harriet Martineau bore practical fruit. In 1858 he issued a new edition of her novel ' Deerbrook,' as well as her ' Suggestions towards the future Government of India.' These were followed by pamphlets respectively on the ' Endowed Schools of Ireland ' and ' England and her Soldiers,' and in 1861 by her well-known 'Household Education.' Subsequently he published her autobiography, the greater part of which she had caused to be put into type and to be kept in readiness for circulation as soon as her death should take place. The firm also undertook the publication of the many tracts and pamphlets in which William Ellis, the zealous disciple of John Stuart Mill, urged improved methods of education during the middle years of the century. To a like category belonged Madame Venturi's translation of Mazzini's works, which Smith, Elder, & Co. issued in six volumes between 1864 and 1870.

At the same period as he became Miss Martineau's publisher there began Smith's interesting connection with Mrs. Gaskell, which was likewise due to Charlotte Brontë. Late in 1855 Mrs. Gaskell set to work, at the request of Charlotte Brontë's father, on his daughter's life. She gleaned many particulars from Smith and his mother, and naturally requested him to publish the book, which proved to be one of the best biographies in the language. But its publication (in 1857) involved him in unwonted anxieties. Mrs. Gaskell deemed it a point of conscience to attribute, for reasons that she gave in detail, the ruin of Miss Brontë's brother Branwell to the machinations of a lady, to whose children he had acted as tutor. As soon as Smith learned Mrs. Gaskell's intention he warned her of the possible consequences. The warning passed unheeded. The offensive particulars appeared in the biography, and, as soon as it was published, an action for libel was threatened. Mrs. Gaskell was travelling in France at the moment, and her address was unknown. Smith investigated the matter for himself, and, perceiving that Mrs. Gaskell's statements were not legally justifiable, withdrew the book from circulation. In later editions the offending passages were suppressed. Sir James Stephen, on behalf of friends of the lady whose character was aspersed, took part in the negotiations, and on their conclusion handsomely commended Smith's conduct.

IV

In the opening months of 1859 Smith turned his attention to an entirely new publishing venture. He then laid the foundations of the ' Cornhill Magazine,' the first of the three great literary edifices which he reared by his own effort. It was his intimacy with Thackeray that led Smith to establish the ' Cornhill Magazine.' The periodical originally was designed with the sole object of offering the public a novel by Thackeray in serial instalments combined with a liberal allowance of other first-rate literary matter. In February 1859 Smith offered Thackeray the liberal terms of 350*l.* for a monthly instalment of a novel, which was to be completed in twelve numbers. The profits on separate publication of the work, after the first edition, were to be equally divided between author and publisher. Thackeray agreed to these conditions; but it was only after Smith had failed in various quarters to secure a fitting editor for the new venture—Tom Hughes was among those who were invited and declined—that he appealed to Thackeray to fill the editorial chair. He proposed a salary of 1,000*l.* a year. Thackeray consented to take the post on the understanding that Smith should assist him in business details. Thackeray christened the periodical 'The Cornhill' after its publishing home, and chose for its cover the familiar design by Godfrey Sykes, a South Kensington art student. The 'Cornhill' was launched on January 1, 1860. The first number reached a sale of one hundred and twenty thousand copies. Although so vast a circulation was not maintained, the magazine for many years enjoyed a prosperity that was without precedent in the annals of English periodical publications.

Thackeray's fame and genius rendered services to the 'Cornhill' that are not easy to exaggerate. He was not merely editor, but by far the largest contributor. Besides his novel of 'Lovel the Widower,' which ran through the early numbers, he supplied each month a delightful 'Roundabout Paper,' which was deservedly paid at the high rate of twelve guineas a page. But identified as Thackeray was with the success of the 'Cornhill'—an identification which Smith acknowledged by doubling his editorial salary—Thackeray would have been the first to admit that the practical triumphs of the enterprise were largely the fruits of the energy, resourcefulness, and liberality of the proprietor. There was no writer of eminence, there was hardly an artist of distinguished merit (for the magazine was richly illustrated), whose co-operation Smith, when planning with Thackeray the early numbers, did not seek, often in a personal interview, on terms of exceptional munificence. Associates of earlier date, like John Ruskin and George Henry Lewes among authors, and Millais, Leighton, and Richard Doyle among artists, were requisitioned as a matter of course. Lewes was an indefatigable contributor from the start. Ruskin wrote a paper on ' Sir Joshua and Holbein ' for the third number, but Ruskin's subsequent participation brought home to Smith and his editor the personal embarrassments inevitable in the conduct of a popular magazine by an editor and a publisher, both of whom were rich in eminent literary friends. When, later in the first year, Ruskin sent for serial issue a treatise on political economy, entitled ' Unto this Last,' his doctrine was seen to be too deeply tainted with socialistic heresy to conciliate subscribers. Smith published four articles and then informed the author that the editor could accept no more. Smith afterwards issued ' Unto this Last' in a separate volume, but the forced cessation of the papers in the magazine impaired the old cordiality of intercourse between author and publisher.

The magazine necessarily brought Smith into relations with many notable writers and artists of whom he had known little or nothing before. He visited Tennyson and offered him 5,000*l.* for a poem of the length of the ' Idylls of the King.' This was declined, but ' Tithonus ' appeared in the second number. Another poet, a friend of Thackeray, who first came into relations with Smith through the ' Cornhill,' was Mrs. Browning, whose ' Great God Pan,' illustrated by Leighton, adorned the seventh number (July 1860). The artist Frederick Walker, who was afterwards on intimate terms with Smith, casually called at the office as a lad and asked for work on the magazine. His capacities were tested without delay, and he illustrated the greater part of 'Philip, the second novel that Thackeray wrote for the 'Cornhill.' It was Leighton who suggested to Smith that he should give a trial as an illustrator to George Du Maurier, who quickly became one of the literary and artistic acquaintances in whose society he most delighted.

Two essayists of different type, although each was endowed with distinctive style and exceptional insight, Fitzjames Stephen and Matthew Arnold, were among the most interesting of the early contributors to the 'Cornhill.' Stephen contributed two articles at the end of 1860, and through the years 1861–3 wrote as many as eight annually —on literary, philosophical, and social subjects.

Matthew Arnold's work for the magazine was of great value to its reputation. His essay on Eugénie de Guérin (June 1863) had the distinction of bearing at the end the writer's name. That was a distinction almost unique in those days, for the 'Cornhill' then as a rule jealously guarded the anonymity of its authors. On June 16, 1863, Arnold wrote to his mother of his Oxford lecture on Heine : 'I have had two applications for the lecture from magazines, but I shall print it, if I can, in the "Cornhill," because it both pays best and has much the largest circle of readers. "Eugénie de Guérin" seems to be much liked.'[1] The lecture on Heine appeared in the 'Cornhill' for October 1863. The hearty welcome given his articles by the conductors of the 'Cornhill' inspired Arnold with a 'sense of gratitude and surprise.' A paper by him entitled 'My Countrymen' in February 1866 'made a good deal of talk.' There followed his fine lectures on 'Celtic Literature,' and the articles which were reissued by Smith, Elder, & Co. in the characteristic volumes entitled respectively 'Culture and Anarchy' (1868), 'St.

[1] *Letters of M. Arnold*, ed. G. W. E. Russell, i. 195.

Paul and Protestantism' (1861), and 'Literature and Dogma' (1871).

With both Fitzjames Stephen and Matthew Arnold Smith maintained almost from their first introduction to the 'Cornhill' close personal intercourse. He especially enjoyed his intimacy with Matthew Arnold, whose idiosyncrasies charmed him as much as his light-hearted banter. He published for Arnold nearly all his numerous prose works, and showed every regard for him and his family. While Arnold was residing in the country at a later period, Smith provided a room for him at his publishing offices in Waterloo Place when he had occasion to stay the night in town.[1]

Chief among novelists whom the inauguration of the 'Cornhill Magazine' brought permanently to Smith's side was Anthony Trollope. He had already made some reputation with novels dealing with clerical life, and when in October 1859 he offered his services to Thackeray as a writer of short stories—he was then personally unknown to both Smith and Thackeray—Smith promptly (on October 26) offered him 1,000l. for the copyright of a clerical novel to run serially from the first number, provided only that the first portion should be forwarded by December 12. Trollope was already engaged on an Irish story, but a clerical novel would alone satisfy Smith. In the result Trollope began 'Framley Parsonage,' and Smith invited Millais to illustrate it. Thackeray courteously accorded

---

[1] Cf. Arnold's *Letters*, ed. G. W. E. Russell. On May 31, 1871, Arnold writes to his mother: 'I have come in to dine with George Smith in order to meet old Charles Lever' (ii. 57). On October 2, 1874, he writes again: 'I have been two nights splendidly put up at G. Smith's [residence in South Kensington], and shall be two nights there next week. I like now to dine anywhere rather than at a club, and G. Smith has a capital billiard table, and after dinner we play billiards, which I like very much, and it suits me' (ii. 117). Writing from his home at Cobham to his sister on December 27, 1886, Arnold notes: 'We were to have dined with the George Smiths at Walton to-night, but can neither go nor telegraph. The roads are impassable and the telegraph wires broken' (ii. 360).

the first place in the first number (January 1860) to the initial instalment of Trollope's novel. Trollope was long a mainstay of the magazine, and his private relations with Smith were very intimate. In August 1861 he began a second story, entitled ' The Struggles of Brown, Jones, and Robinson,' a humorous satire on the ways of trade, which proved a failure. Six hundred pounds was paid for it, but Smith made no complaint, merely remarking to the author that he did not think it equal to his usual work. In September 1862 Trollope offered reparation by sending to the ' Cornhill ' ' The Small House at Allington.' Finally, in 1866-7, Trollope's ' Claverings ' appeared in the magazine ; for this he received 2,800l. ' Whether much or little,' Trollope wrote, ' it was offered by the proprietor, and paid in a single cheque.' When contrasting his experiences as contributor to other periodicals with those he enjoyed as contributor to the ' Cornhill,' Trollope wrote, ' What I wrote for the " Cornhill Magazine " I always wrote at the instigation of Mr. Smith.' [1]

George Henry Lewes had introduced Smith to George Eliot soon after their union in 1854. Her voice and conversation always filled Smith with admiration, and when the Leweses settled at North Bank in 1863 he was rarely absent from her Sunday receptions until they ceased at Lewes's death in 1878. Early in 1862 she read to him a portion of the manuscript of ' Romola,' and he gave practical proof of his faith in her genius by offering her 10,000l. for the right of issuing the novel serially in the ' Cornhill Magazine,' and of subsequent separate publication. The reasonable condition was attached that the story should first be distributed over sixteen numbers of the ' Cornhill.' George Eliot agreed to the terms, but embarrassments followed. She deemed it necessary to divide the story into twelve parts instead of the stipulated

[1] Anthony Trollope's *Autobiography*, i. 231.

sixteen. From a business point of view the change, as the authoress frankly acknowledged, amounted to a serious breach of contract, but she was deaf to both Smith's and Lewes's appeal to her to respect the original agreement. She offered, however, in consideration of her obstinacy, to accept the reduced remuneration of 7,000*l.* The story was not completed by the authoress when she settled this serial division. Ultimately she discovered that she had miscalculated the length which the story would reach, and, after all, 'Romola' ran through fourteen numbers of the magazine (July 1862 to August 1863). Leighton was chosen by Smith to illustrate the story. The whole transaction was not to Smith's pecuniary advantage, but the cordiality of his relations with the authoress remained unchecked. Her story of 'Brother Jacob,' which appeared in the 'Cornhill' in July 1864, was forwarded to him as a free gift. Afterwards, in 1866, she sent him the manuscript of 'Felix Holt,' but after reading it he did not feel justified in accepting it at the price of 5,000*l.*, which George Eliot or Lewes set upon it.

Meanwhile, in March 1862 the 'Cornhill' had suffered a severe blow through the sudden resignation of the editor, Thackeray. He found the thorns in the editorial cushion too sharp-pointed for his sensitive nature. Smith keenly regretted his decision to retire, but when Thackeray took public farewell of his post in a brief article in the magazine for April ('To Contributors and Correspondents,' dated March 18, 1862), the novelist stated that, though editor no more, he hoped 'long to remain to contribute to my friend's magazine.' This hope was realised up to the moment of Thackeray's unexpected death on December 23, 1863. His final 'Roundabout Paper'—'Strange to say on Club Paper'—appeared in the magazine for the preceding November, and he had nearly completed his novel, 'Denis Duval,' which was to form the chief serial story in the 'Cornhill' during 1864. Nor was Thackeray the only member of his family who was in these early days a contributor to the magazine. Thackeray's daughter (Mrs. Richmond Ritchie) had contributed a paper called ' Little Scholars ' to the fifth number while her father was editor, and in 1862, after his withdrawal, Smith accepted her novel, 'The Story of Elizabeth,' the first of many from the same pen to appear serially in the ' Cornhill.' Thackeray's death naturally caused Smith intense pain. He at once did all he could to aid his friend's daughters. In consultation with their friends, Herman Merivale, (Sir) Henry Cole, and Fitzjames Stephen, he purchased their rights in their father's books, and by arrangement with Thackeray's other publishers, Chapman & Hall and Bradbury & Evans, who owned part shares in some of his works, acquired the whole of Thackeray's literary property. He subsequently published no less than seven complete collections of Thackeray's works in different forms, the earliest—the ' Library Edition ' in twenty-two volumes—appearing in 1867-9. Thackeray's daughters stayed with Smith's family at Brighton in the early days of their sorrow, and he was gratified to receive a letter from Thackeray's mother, Mrs. Carmichael Smyth, thanking him for his resourceful kindness (August 24, 1864). ' I rejoice,' she wrote, ' that such a friend is assured to my grandchildren.' Her expressions were well justified. Until Smith's death there subsisted a close friendship between him and Thackeray's elder daughter (Mrs. Ritchie), and he was fittingly godfather of Thackeray's granddaughter (Mrs. Ritchie's daughter).

On Thackeray's withdrawal from the editorship the office was temporarily placed in commission. Smith invited Lewes and Mr. Frederick Greenwood, a young journalist who had contributed to the second number a striking paper, 'An Essay without End,' to aid himself in conducting the magazine. This arrangement lasted two years. In 1864 Lewes retired, and Mr. Greenwood filled the editorial chair alone until his absorption in other work in 1868 compelled him to delegate most of his functions to Dutton Cook.

A singular and somewhat irritating experience befell Smith as proprietor in 1869. In April 1868 a gossiping article called 'Don Ricardo' narrated some adventures of 'General Plantagenet Harrison,' a name which the writer believed to be wholly imaginary. In June 1869 Smith was proceeded against for libel by one who actually bore that designation. It seemed difficult to treat the grievance seriously, but the jury returned a verdict for the plaintiff, and assessed the damages at 50l. In March 1871 Mr. Dutton Cook withdrew from the editorship of the 'Cornhill.' Thereupon Mr. Leslie Stephen became editor, and Smith practically left the whole direction in the new editor's hands.

Until Mr. Stephen's advent Smith had comparatively rarely left the helm of his fascinating venture. His contributor Trollope always maintained that throughout the sixties Smith's hand exclusively guided the fortunes of the 'Cornhill.' [1] It was certainly he alone who contrived to secure most of the important contributions during the later years of the decade. On Thackeray's death he invited Charles Dickens to supply for the February number of 1864 an article 'In Memoriam.' Dickens promptly acceded, and declined to accept payment for his article. It was to Smith personally that George Eliot presented her story of 'Brother Jacob,' which appeared in July following. A year before, he had undertaken the publication of two novels, 'Sylvia's Lovers' and 'A Dark Night's Work,' by his acquaintance of earlier days, Mrs. Gaskell, and at the same time he arranged for the serial issue in the magazine of 'Cousin Phillis,' a new novel (1863–4), as well as of her final novel of 'Wives and Daughters.'

[1] Anthony Trollope's *Autobiography*, ii. 125.

The last began in August 1864, and ended in January 1866. With the sum of 2,000*l.* which was paid for the work, Mrs. Gaskell purchased a country house at Holybourne, near Alton, where, before she had completed the manuscript of her story, she died suddenly on November 12, 1865. The relations existing between Smith and Mrs. Gaskell and her daughters at the time of her death were of the friendliest, and his friendship with the daughters proved lifelong. As in the case of Thackeray's works, he soon purchased the copyrights of all Mrs. Gaskell's books, and issued many attractive collections of them. He was also responsible for the serial appearance in the 'Cornhill' of Wilkie Collins's 'Armadale,' which was continued through the exceptional number of twenty parts (November 1864 to June 1866) ; of Miss Thackeray's 'Village on the Cliff,' which appeared in 1866-7 ; of three stories by Charles Lever—'The Bramleighs of Bishop's Folly,' 'That Boy of Norcott's,' and 'Lord Kilgobbin'—which followed each other in almost uninterrupted succession through the magazine from 1867 to 1872 ; of Charles Reade's 'Put yourself in his Place,' which was commenced in 1869 ; and of George Meredith's 'Adventures of Harry Richmond,' which began in 1870.

Most of these writers were the publisher's personal friends. Although Reade's boisterous personality did not altogether attract Smith in private life, he was fully alive to his transparent sincerity. Apart from the magazine, he transacted much publishing business with Wilkie Collins and with Miss Thackeray (Mrs. Ritchie). He published (separately from the magazine) all Miss Thackeray's novels. For a time he took over Wilkie Collins's books, issuing a collective edition of them between 1865 and 1870. But this connection was not lasting. Smith refused in the latter year to accede to Collins's request to publish a new work of his in sixpenny parts, and at the close of 1874 Collins transferred all his publications (save those of which the copyright had been acquired by Smith, Elder, & Co.) to the firm of Chatto & Windus. Smith was not wholly unversed in the methods of publication which Collins had invited him to pursue. He had in 1866 purchased the manuscript of Trollope's 'Last Chronicles of Barset' for 3,000l., and had issued it by way of experiment in sixpenny parts. The result did not encourage a repetition of the plan.

One of the pleasantest features of the early history of the 'Cornhill' was the monthly dinner which Smith gave the contributors for the first year at his house in Gloucester Square. Thackeray was usually the chief guest, and he and Smith spared no pains to give the meetings every convivial advantage. On one occasion Trollope thoughtlessly described the entertainment to Edmund Yates, who was at feud with Thackeray, and Yates wrote for a New York paper an ill-natured description of Smith in his character of host, which was quoted in the 'Saturday Review.' Thackeray made a sufficiently effective retaliation in a 'Roundabout Paper' entitled 'On Screens in Dining-rooms.' The hospitality which Smith offered his 'Cornhill' coadjutors and other friends took a new shape in 1863, when he acquired a house at Hampstead called Oak Hill Lodge. For some ten years he resided there during the summer, and spent the winter at Brighton, travelling to and from London each day. Partly on Thackeray's suggestion, at the beginning of each summer from 1863 onwards, there was issued by Mr. and Mrs. George Smith a general invitation to their friends to dine at Hampstead on any Friday they chose, without giving notice. This mode of entertainment proved thoroughly successful. The number of guests varied greatly : once they reached as many as forty. Thackeray, Millais, and Leech were among the earliest arrivals ; afterwards Trollope rarely failed, and Wilkie Collins was often present. Turgenieff, the Russian novelist, was a guest on one occasion.

Subsequently Du Maurier, a regular attendant, drew an amusing menu-card, in which Mrs. Smith was represented driving a reindeer in a sleigh which was laden with provisions in a packing-case. Few authors or artists who gained reputation in the seventh decade of the nineteenth century failed to enjoy Smith's genial hospitality at Hampstead on one or other Friday during that period. Under the auspices of his numerous literary friends, he was admitted to two well-known clubs during the first half of the same decade. In 1861 he joined the Reform Club, for which Sir Arthur Buller, a friend of Thackeray, proposed him, and Thackeray himself seconded him. In 1865 he was elected to the Garrick Club on the nomination of Anthony Trollope and Wilkie Collins, supported by Charles Reade, Tom Taylor, (Sir) Theodore Martin, and many others. He also became a member of the Cosmopolitan Club.

V

The general business of Smith, Elder, & Co. through the sixties was extremely prosperous. In 1861 an additional office was taken in the West End of London at 45 Pall Mall, nearly opposite Marlborough House. The shock of the Mutiny was ended, the Indian trade was making enormous strides. Smith, Elder, & Co. had supplied some of the scientific plant for the construction of the Ganges canal, and in 1860 they celebrated the accomplishment of the great task by bringing out a formidable quarto, Sir Proby Thomas Cautley's 'Report of the Construction of the Ganges Canal, with an Atlas of Plans.' The publishing affairs of the concern were meanwhile entirely satisfactory. The success of the 'Cornhill' had given them a new spur. It had attracted to the firm s banner not merely almost every author of repute, but almost every artist of rising fame. Not the least interesting publication to which the magazine gave rise was the volume called 'The Cornhill Gallery : 100 Engravings,' which appeared in 1864. Portions of it were reissued in 1866 in three volumes, containing respectively engravings after drawings made for the 'Cornhill' by Leighton, Walker, and Millais. Ruskin's pen was still prolific and popular, and the many copyrights that had been recently acquired proved valuable.

With characteristic energy Smith now set foot in a new field of congenial activity, where he thought to turn to enhanced advantage the special position and opportunities that he commanded in the world of letters. The firm already owned two weekly newspapers of somewhat special character—the 'Homeward Mail' and 'Overland Mail'—and Smith had been told that he could acquire without difficulty a third periodical, 'The Queen.' But it was his ambition, if he added to the firm's newspaper property at all, to inaugurate a daily journal of an original type. The leading papers paid small attention to literature and art, and often presented the news of the day heavily and unintelligently. There was also a widespread suspicion that musical and theatrical notices, and such few reviews of books as were admitted to the daily press, were not always disinterested. It was views like these, which Smith held strongly, that had prompted in 1854 Thackeray's scheme of a daily sheet of frank and just criticism to be entitled 'Fair Play.' That scheme had been partly responsible for Thackeray's 'Roundabout Papers' in the 'Cornhill Magazine,' but they necessarily only touched its fringe. Thackeray's original proposal was recalled to Smith's mind in 1863 by a cognate suggestion then made to him by Mr. Frederick Greenwood. Mr. Greenwood thought to start a new journal that should reproduce the form and spirit of Canning's 'Anti-Jacobin.' After much discussion the plan of a new evening newspaper was finally settled by Smith and Mr. Greenwood. Men of literary ability and unquestioned independence were to be enlisted in its service. News was to be reported in plain English, but the greater part of the paper was to be devoted to original articles on 'public affairs, literature, the arts, and all the influences which strengthen or dissipate society.' The aim was to bring into daily journalism as much sound thought, knowledge, and style as were possible to its conditions, and to counteract corrupting influences. No books published by Smith, Elder, & Co. were to be reviewed. The advertisement department was to be kept free from abuses. Quack medicine vendors and money-lenders were to be excluded.

Smith himself christened the projected paper 'The Pall Mall Gazette,' in allusion to the journal that Thackeray invented for the benefit of Arthur Pendennis. To Mr. Greenwood's surprise Smith appointed him editor. King, Smith's partner, agreed that the firm should undertake the pecuniary responsibilities. A warehouse at the river end of Salisbury Street, Strand, on the naked foreshore of the Thames, was acquired to serve as a printing-office, and a small dwelling-house some doors nearer the Strand in the same street was rented for editorial and publishing purposes. Late in 1864 a copy of the paper was written and printed by way of testing the general machinery. Although independence in all things had been adopted as the paper's watchword, King, who was a staunch Conservative, was dissatisfied with the political tone of the first number, which in his opinion inclined to Liberalism. He summarily vetoed the firm's association with the enterprise. Smith had gone too far to withdraw, and promptly accepted the sole ownership.

The first number of the paper was issued from Salisbury Street on February 7, 1865, the day of the opening of parliament. It was in form a large quarto, consisting of eight pages, and the price was twopence. The leading article by the editor dealt sympathetically with 'the

Queen's seclusion.' The only signed article was a long letter by Anthony Trollope on the American civil war—a strong appeal on behalf of the North. The unsigned articles included an instalment of 'Friends in Council,' by Sir Arthur Helps; an article entitled 'Ladies at Law,' by John Ormsby; and the first of a series of 'Letters from Sir Pitt Crawley, Bart., to his nephew on his entering Parliament,' by 'Pitt Crawley' the pseudonym of Sir Reginald Palgrave. There were three of the 'occasional notes' which were to form a special feature of the paper. One page—the last—was filled with advertisements. It was not a strong number. The public proved indifferent, and only four thousand copies were sold.

Smith found no difficulty in collecting round him a brilliant band of professional writers and men in public life who were ready to place their pens at the disposal of the 'Pall Mall Gazette.' Many of them had already contributed to the 'Cornhill.' The second number afforded conspicuous proof of the success with which he and Mr. Greenwood had recruited their staff. In that number Fitzjames Stephen, who had long been a regular contributor to the 'Cornhill,' began a series of leading articles and other contributions which for five years proved of the first importance to the character of the paper. Until 1869 Fitzjames Stephen wrote far more than half the leading articles; in 1868 he wrote as many as two-thirds. When he went to India in 1869 his place as leader writer was to some extent filled by Sir Henry Maine; but during his voyage home from India in 1872–1873 Fitzjames Stephen wrote, for serial issue in the 'Pall Mall,' masterly articles called 'Liberty, Equality, and Fraternity,' which Smith afterwards published in a volume.

When the 'Pall Mall Gazette' was in its inception, Fitzjames Stephen moreover introduced Smith to his brother, Mr. Leslie Stephen, with a view to his writing in

the paper. Like Fitzjames's first contribution, Mr. Leslie
Stephen's first contribution appeared in the second number,
and it marked the commencement of Mr. Leslie Stephen's
long relationship with Smith and his firm, which was
strengthened by Mr. Stephen's marriage in 1867 to
Thackeray's younger daughter (she died in 1875), and
was always warmly appreciated by Smith. George Henry
Lewes's versatility was once again at Smith's command,
and a salary for general assistance of 300*l.* was paid him
in the first year. Before the end of the first month the
ranks of the writers for the 'Pall Mall' were joined by
R. H. Hutton, Sir John Kaye, Charles Lever, John
Addington Symonds, and, above all, by Matthew James
Higgins. Higgins was a friend of Thackeray, and a contributor to the 'Cornhill;' his terse outspoken letters to
the 'Times' bearing the signature of 'Jacob Omnium'
were, at the time of their appearance, widely appreciated.
He was long an admirable compiler of occasional notes
for the 'Pall Mall,' and led controversies there with great
adroitness. He was almost as strong a pillar of the journal's
sturdy independence in its early life as Fitzjames Stephen
himself. Twice in March 1865, once in April, and once
in May, George Eliot contributed attractive articles on
social subjects.[1] Smith, who had persuaded Trollope
to lend a hand, sent him to Exeter Hall to report his impressions of the May meetings ; but the fulfilment of the
commission taxed Trollope's patience beyond endurance,
and the proposal only resulted in a single paper called
'A Zulu in search of a Religion.' Much help was regularly given by Lord and Lady Strangford, both of whom
Smith found charming companions socially. Among
occasional contributors were Mr. Goschen, (Sir) Henry
Drummond Wolff, Tom Hughes, Lord Houghton, Mr.

---

[1] George Eliot's articles were : 'A Word for the Germans' (March 7),
'Servants' Logic' (March 17), 'Little Falsehoods' (April 3), 'Modern
Housekeeping' (May 13).

John Morley, and Charles Reade. Thackeray's friend, James Hannay, was summoned from Edinburgh to assist in the office.

But, despite so stalwart a phalanx of powerful writers, the public was slow to recognise the paper's merits. The strict anonymity which the writers preserved did not give their contributions the benefit of their general reputation, and the excellence of the writing largely escaped recognition. In April 1865 the sales hardly averaged 613 a day, while the amount received for advertisements was often only 3*l.* Smith's interest in the venture was intense. In every department of the paper he expended his personal energy. For the first two years he kept with his own hand ' the contributors' ledger ' and ' the register of contributors,' and one day every week he devoted many hours at home to posting up these books and writing out and despatching the contributors' cheques. From the first he taxed his ingenuity for methods whereby to set the paper on a stable footing. Since the public were slow to appreciate the ' Pall Mall ' of an afternoon, he, for three weeks in the second month of its existence, supplied a morning edition. But buyers and advertisers proved almost shyer of a morning than of an evening, and the morning issue was promptly suspended. Smith's spirits often drooped in the face of the obduracy of the public, and he contemplated abandoning the enterprise. His sanguine temperament never prevented him from frankly acknowledging defeat when cool judgment could set no other interpretation on the position of affairs. Happily in the course of 1866 the tide showed signs of turning. In the spring of that year Mr. Greenwood requested his brother to contribute three papers called ' A Night in a Casual Ward : by an Amateur Casual.' General interest was roused, and the circulation of the paper slowly rose. Soon afterwards an exposure of a medical quack, Dr. Hunter, who was advertising a cure for consumption, led to an action for libel against the publisher. Smith, who thoroughly enjoyed the excitement of the struggle, justified the comment, and adduced in its support the testimony of many distinguished members of the medical profession. The jury gave the plaintiff one farthing by way of damages. The case attracted wide attention, and leading doctors and others showed their opinon of Smith's conduct by presenting him after the trial with a silver vase and salver in recognition, they declared, of his courageous de-fence of the right of honest criticism. A year later the victory was won, and a profitable period in the fortunes of the 'Pall Mall Gazette' set in. In 1867 the construction of the Thames Embankment rendered necessary the de-molition of the old printing-office, and more convenient premises were found in Northumberland Street, Strand. On April 29, 1868, Smith celebrated the arrival of the favouring breeze by a memorable dinner to contributors at Greenwich. The number of pages of the paper was increased to sixteen, and for a short time in 1869 the price was reduced to a penny, but it was soon raised to the original twopence. In 1870 the 'Pall Mall Gazette' was the first to announce in this country the issue of the battle of Sedan and Napoleon III's surrender.

The less adventurous publishing work which Smith and his partner were conducting at Cornhill at this time benefited by the growth of Smith's circle of friends at the office of his newspaper. Sir Arthur Helps, who was writing occasionally for the 'Pall Mall Gazette,' was Clerk of the Council and in confidential relations with Queen Victoria. Smith published a new series of his 'Friends in Council' in 1869. At Helps's suggestion Smith, Elder, & Co. were invited in 1867 to print two volumes in which Queen Victoria was deeply interested. Very early in the year there was delivered to Smith the manuscript of the Queen's 'Leaves from the Journal of our Life in the Highlands, 1848–1861.' It was originally intended to print only a few copies for circulation among the Queen's friends. Smith was enjoined to take every precaution for secrecy in the preparation of the book. The manager of the firm's printing-office in Little Green Arbour Court set up the type with a single assistant in a room which was kept under lock and key, and was always occupied by one or other of them while the work was in progress. The Queen expressed her satisfaction at the way in which the secret was kept. After forty copies had been printed and bound for her private use, she was persuaded to permit an edition to be prepared for the public. This appeared in December 1867. It was in great request, and reprints were numerous. Meanwhile, at Helps's suggestion, Smith prepared for publication under very similar conditions General Grey's 'Early Years of the Prince Consort,' which was written under the Queen's supervision. A first edition of five thousand copies appeared in August 1867. There naturally followed the commission to undertake the issue of the later 'Life of the Prince Consort,' which Sir Theodore Martin, on Helps's recommendation, took up after General Grey's death. Smith was a lifelong admirer of Sir Theodore Martin's wife, Helen Faucit, the distinguished actress, whose portrait he had published in his second publication (of 1844), Mrs. Wilson's ' Our Actresses.' He already knew Theodore Martin, and the engagement to publish his biography of Prince Albert, which came out in five volumes between 1874 and 1880, rendered the relations with the Martins very close. To Sir Theodore, Smith was until his death warmly attached. In 1884 Smith brought out a second instalment of the Queen's journal, ' More Leaves from the Journal of a Life in the Highlands, 1862-1882,' which, like its forerunner, enjoyed wide popularity.

VI

In 1868 a new act in the well-filled drama of Smith's business career opened. He determined in that year to retire from the foreign agency and banking work of the firm, and to identify himself henceforth solely with the publishing branch. Arrangements were made whereby his partner, King, took over the agency and banking business, which he carried on under the style of 'Henry S. King & Co.' at the old premises in Cornhill and at the more recently acquired offices in Pall Mall, while Smith opened, under the old style of 'Smith, Elder, & Co.,' new premises, to which the publishing branch was transferred, to be henceforth under his sole control. He chose for Smith, Elder, & Co.'s new home a private residence, 15 Waterloo Place, then in the occupation of a partner in the banking firm of Herries, Farquhar, & Co. It was not the most convenient building that could be found for his purpose, and was only to be acquired at a high cost. But he had somewhat fantastically set his heart upon it, and he adapted it to his needs as satisfactorily as he could. In January 1869 he with many members of the Cornhill staff permanently removed to Smith, Elder, & Co.'s new abode.

The increase of leisure and the diminution of work which the change brought with it had a very different effect on Smith's health from what was anticipated. The sudden relaxation affected his constitution disastrously, and for the greater part of the next year and a half he was seriously incapacitated by illness. Long absences in Scotland and on the continent became necessary, and it was not till 1870 was well advanced that his vigour was restored. He characteristically celebrated the return of health by inviting the children of his numerous friends to witness with him and his family the Covent Garden pantomime at Christmas 1870-71. The party exceeded ninety in number, and he engaged for his guests, after much negotiation, the whole of the first row of the dress circle. Millais's children filled the central places.

In 1870 Smith's energy revived in its pristine abundance, and, finding inadequate scope in his publishing business, it sought additional outlets elsewhere. Early in the year he resolved to make a supreme effort to produce a morning paper. A morning edition of the 'Pall Mall Gazette' was devised anew on a grand scale. In form it followed the lines of the 'Times.' Smith threw himself into the project with exceptional ardour. He spent every night at the office supervising every detail of the paper's production. But the endeavour failed, and, after four months of heavy toil and large expenditure, the enterprise was abandoned. Meanwhile the independent evening issue of the 'Pall Mall' continued to make satisfactory progress. But the discouraging experience of the morning paper did not daunt his determination to obtain occupation and investments for capital supplemental to that with which his publishing business provided him. Later in 1870 he went into partnership with Mr. Arthur Bilbrough, as a shipowner and underwriter, at 36 Fenchurch Street. The firm was known as Smith, Bilbrough, & Co. Smith joined Lloyd's in 1871, but underwriting did not appeal much to him, and he soon gave it up. On the other hand, the width of his interest and intelligence rendered the position of a shipowner wholly congenial. His operations in that capacity were vigorously pursued, and were attended by success. The firm acquired commanding interests in thirteen or fourteen sailing vessels of large tonnage, and they built in 1874 on new principles, which were afterwards imitated, a cargo boat of great dimensions, which Smith christened 'Old Kensington,' after Miss Thackeray's well-known novel. The book had just passed serially through the 'Cornhill.' Sailors who were not aware of the source of the name raised a superstitious objection to the epithet 'Old,' but Smith, although sympathetic, would not give way, and cherished a personal pride in the vessel. When in 1879 he resigned his partnership in Smith, Bilbrough, & Co., he still retained his share in the 'Old Kensington.' Until 1879, when he withdrew from the shipping business, he spent the early part of each morning at its office in Fenchurch Street and the rest of the working day at Waterloo Place, where, despite his numerous other interests, he spared no pains to develop his publishing connection. His settlement in Waterloo Place almost synchronised with the opening of his cordial relations with Robert Browning. Smith had met Browning casually in early life, and Browning's friend Chorley had asked Smith to take over the poet's publications from his original publisher, Moxon ; but, at the moment, the financial position of Smith, Elder, & Co. did not justify him in accepting the proposal. In 1868 Browning himself asked him to undertake a collective issue of his 'Poetical Works,' and he produced an edition in six volumes. Later in the same year Browning placed in Smith's hands the manuscript of 'The Ring and the Book.' He paid the poet 1,250l. for the right of publication during five years. The great work appeared in four monthly volumes, which were issued respectively in November and December 1868, and January and February 1869. Of the first two volumes, the edition consisted of three thousand copies each ; but the sale was not rapid, and of the last two volumes only two thousand were printed. Browning presented Mrs. Smith with the manuscript. Thenceforth Smith was, for the rest of Browning's life, his only publisher, and he also took over the works of Mrs. Browning from Chapman & Hall. The two men were soon on very intimate terms. In 1871 he accepted Browning's poem of 'Hervé Riel' for the 'Cornhill Magazine.' Browning had asked him to buy

E

it so that he might forward a subscription to the fund for the relief of the people of Paris after the siege. Smith sent the poet 100*l.* by return of post. Fifteen separate volumes of new verse by Browning appeared with Smith, Elder, & Co.'s imprint between 1871 and the date of the poet's death late in 1889. In 1888, too, Smith began a new collected edition which extended to seventeen volumes, and yielded handsome gains (in 1896 he brought out a cheaper complete collection in two volumes). He thus had the satisfaction of presiding over the fortunes of Browning's works when, for the first time in his long life, they brought their author substantial profit. Though Browning, like many other eminent English poets, was a man of affairs, he left his publishing concerns entirely in Smith's hands. No cloud ever darkened their private or professional intercourse. The poet's last letter to his publisher, dated from Asolo, September 27, 1889, contained the words 'and now to our immediate business [the proofs of the volume 'Asolando' were going through the press at the moment], which is only to keep thanking you for your constant goodness, present and future.'[1] Almost the last words of Browning on his deathbed were to bid his son seek George Smith's advice whenever he had need of good counsel. Smith superintended the arrangements for Browning's funeral in Westminster Abbey on December 31, 1889, and was justly accorded a place among the pall-bearers.

While the association with Browning was growing close Smith reluctantly parted company with another great author whose works he had published continuously from the start of each in life. A rift in the intimacy between Ruskin and Smith had begun when the issue of ' Unto this Last ' in the ' Cornhill ' was broken off in 1861, and the death of Ruskin's father in 1864 severed a strong link in the chain that originally united them. But more

[1] Mrs. Orr's *Life of Robert Browning,* p. 417.

than ten years passed before the alienation became complete. For no author did the firm publish a greater number of separate volumes. During the forties they published three volumes by Ruskin; during the fifties no less than twenty-six; during the sixties as many as eight, including 'The Crown of Wild Olive,' 'Sesame and Lilies,' and 'Queen of the Air.' In the early seventies Ruskin's pen was especially active. In 1871 he entrusted Smith with the first number of 'Fors Clavigera.' In 1872 the firm brought out four new works: 'The Eagle's Nest,' 'Munera Pulveris,' 'Aratra Pentelici,' and 'Michael Angelo and Tintoret.' But by that date Ruskin had matured views about the distribution of books which were out of harmony with existing practice. He wished his volumes to be sold to booksellers at the advertised price without discount and to leave it to them to make what profits they chose in disposing of the books to their customers. Smith was not averse to making the experiment which Ruskin desired, but the booksellers did not welcome the new plan of sale, and the circulation of Ruskin's books declined. Further difficulties followed in regard to reprints of his early masterpieces, 'Modern Painters' and the 'Stones of Venice.' Many of the plates were worn out, and Ruskin hesitated to permit them to be replaced or retouched now that their original engraver, Thomas Lupton, was dead. He desired to limit very strictly the number of copies in the new editions; he announced that the time had come for issuing a final edition of his early works, and pledged himself to suffer no reprint hereafter. These conditions also failed to harmonise with the habitual methods of the publishing business. A breach proved inevitable, and finally Ruskin made other arrangements for the production and publication of his writings. In 1871 he employed Mr. George Allen to aid him personally in preparing and distributing them, and during the course of the next six years gradually transferred to Mr.

Allen all the work that Smith, Elder, & Co. had previously done for him. On September 5, 1878, Ruskin wholly severed his connection with his old publisher by removing all his books from his charge.

Despite many external calls on Smith's attention, the normal work of the publishing firm during the seventies and eighties well maintained its character. The ' Cornhill ' continued to prove a valuable recruiting ground for authors. Mr. Leslie Stephen, after he became editor of the magazine in 1871, welcomed to its pages the early work of many writers who were in due time to add to the stock of permanent English literature. John Addington Symonds wrote many essays and sketches for the magazine, and his chief writings were afterwards published by Smith, Elder, & Co., notably his ' History of the Renaissance,' which came out in seven volumes between 1875 and 1886. Mr. Leslie Stephen himself contributed the critical essays, which were collected under the title of ' Hours in a Library; ' and his ' History of Thought in the Eighteenth Century,' 1876, was among the firm's more important publications. Robert Louis Stevenson was a frequent contributor. Miss Thackeray's ' Old Kensington ' and ' Miss Angel,' Blackmore's ' Erema,' Black's ' Three Feathers ' and ' White Wings,' Mrs. Oliphant's ' Carità ' and ' Within the Precincts,' Mr. W. E. Norris's ' Mdlle. de Mersac,' Mr. Henry James's ' Washington Square,' Mr. Thomas Hardy's ' Far from the Madding Crowd ' and ' The Hand of Ethelberta,' and Mr. James Payn's ' Grape from a Thorn ' were ' Cornhill ' serials while Mr. Stephen guided the fortunes of the periodical, and the majority of them were afterwards issued by Smith, Elder, & Co., in book form. Another change in the *personnel* of the office became necessary on the retirement of Smith Williams in 1875. On the recommendation of Mr. Leslie Stephen, his intimate friend, James Payn the novelist, who had previously edited

'Chambers's Journal,' joined the staff at Waterloo Place as literary adviser in Williams's place. Payn's taste lay in the lighter form of literature. Among the most successful books that he accepted for the firm was F. Anstey's 'Vice Versa.' In 1882, when other duties caused Mr. Leslie Stephen to withdraw from the 'Cornhill,' Payn succeeded him as editor, filling, as before, the position of the firm's 'reader' in addition. With a view to converting the 'Cornhill' into an illustrated repertory of popular fiction, Payn induced Smith to reduce its price to sixpence. The magazine was one of the earliest monthly periodicals to appear at that price. The first number of the 'Cornhill' under the new conditions was issued in July 1883; but the public failed to welcome the innovation, and a return to the old tradition and the old price was made when Payn retired from the editorial chair in 1896. Payn had then fallen into ill-health, and during long years of suffering Smith, whose relations with him were always cordial, showed him touching kindness. While he conducted the magazine, he accepted for the first time serial stories from Dr. Conan Doyle ('The White Company,' 1891), H. S. Merriman, and Mr. Stanley Weyman, and thus introduced to the firm a new generation of popular novelists. Payn's connection with the firm as 'reader' was only terminated by his death in March 1898.

Petty recrimination was foreign to Smith's nature, and the extreme consideration which he paid those who worked with him in mutual sympathy is well illustrated by a story which Payn himself related under veiled names in his 'Literary Recollections.' In 1880 Mr. Shorthouse's 'John Inglesant' was offered to Smith, Elder, & Co., and, by Payn's advice, was rejected. It was accepted by another firm, and obtained great success. A few years afterwards a gossiping paragraph appeared in a newspaper reflecting on the sagacity of Smith, Elder, & Co., in refusing the book. The true facts of the situation had

entirely passed out of Payn's mind, and he regarded the
newspaper's statement as a malicious invention. He
mentioned his intention of publicly denying it. Smith
gently advised him against such a course. Payn insisted
that the remark was damaging both to him and the firm,
and should not be suffered to pass uncorrected. Thereupon Smith quietly pointed out to Payn the true position
of affairs, and called attention to the letter drafted by
Payn himself, in which the firm had refused to undertake
'John Inglesant.' Payn, in reply, expressed his admiration of Smith's magnanimity in forbearing, at the time
that the work he had rejected was achieving a triumphant
circulation at the hands of another firm, to complain by a
single word of his want of foresight. Smith merely
remarked that he was sorry to distress Payn by any
reference to the matter, and should never have mentioned
it had not Payn taken him unawares.

VII

Meanwhile new developments both within and without
the publishing business were in progress. The internal
developments showed that there was no diminution in the
alertness with which modes of extending the scope of the
firm's work were entertained. A series of expensive
éditions de luxe was begun, and a new department of
medical literature was opened. Between October 1878
and September 1879 there was issued an *édition de luxe*
of Thackeray's ' Works ' in twenty-four volumes, to which
two additional volumes of hitherto uncollected writings
were added in 1886. A similarly elaborate reissue of
'Romola,' with Leighton's illustrations, followed in 1880,
and a like reprint of Fielding's ' Works ' in 1882. The last
of these ventures proved the least successful. In 1872
Smith inaugurated a department of medical literature by
purchasing, at the sale of the stock of a firm of medical
publishers, the publishing rights in Ellis's ' Demonstrations

of Anatomy ' and Quain and Wilson's ' Anatomical Plates.' These works formed a nucleus of an extended medical library the chief part of which Smith, Elder, & Co. brought into being between 1873 and 1887   Ernest Hart acted as adviser on the new medical side of the business, and at his suggestion Smith initiated two weekly periodicals dealing with medical topics, which Hart edited. The earlier was the ' London Medical Record,' of which the first number appeared in January 1873 ; the second was the ' Sanitary Record,' of which the first number began in July 1874. After some four years a monthly issue was substituted for the weekly issue in each case, and both were ultimately transferred to other hands. The ' Medical Record ' won a high reputation among medical men through its copious reports of medical practice in foreign countries.   The most notable contributions to medical literature which Smith undertook were, besides Ellis's ' Demonstrations of Anatomy,' Holmes's ' Surgery,' Bristowe's ' Medicine,' Playfair's ' Midwifery,' Marshall's ' Anatomy for Artists,' and Klein's ' Atlas of Histology.' He liked the society of medical men, and while the medical branch of his business was forming he frequently entertained his medical authors at a whist party on Saturday nights in his rooms at Waterloo Place.

Of several new commercial ventures outside the publishing office with which Smith identified himself at this period, one was the Aylesbury Dairy Company, in the direction of which he was for many years associated with his friends Sir Henry Thompson and Tom Hughes. Other mercantile undertakings led to losses, which were faced boldly and cheerfully. It was almost by accident that he engaged in the enterprise which had the most conspicuous and auspicious bearing on his financial position during the last twenty years of his life.   When he was dining with Ernest Hart early in 1872, his host called his attention to some natural aerated water, a specimen of which had just been brought to this country for the first time from the Apollinaris spring in the valley of the Ahr, to the east of the Rhine, between Bonn and Coblenz. Smith, who was impressed by the excellence of the water, remarked half-laughingly that he would like to buy the spring. These casual words subsequently bore important fruit. Negotiations were opened between Smith and Mr. Edward Steinkopff, a German merchant in the City of London, whereby a private company was formed in 1873 for the importation of the Apollinaris water into England, Hart receiving an interest in the profits. A storehouse was taken in the Adelphi, and an office was opened in Regent Street within a short distance of Waterloo Place. As was his custom in all his enterprises, Smith at the outset gave close personal attention to the organisation of the new business, which grew steadily from the first and ultimately reached enormous dimensions. The Apollinaris water sold largely not only in England, but in America, Europe, India, and in the British colonies. The unexpected success of the venture very sensibly augmented Smith's resources. The money he had invested in it amounted to a very few thousand pounds, and this small sum yielded for more than twenty years an increasingly large income which altogether surpassed the returns from his other enterprises. In 1897 the business was profitably disposed of to a public company.

In 1880 Smith lightened his responsibilities in one direction by handing over the 'Pall Mall Gazette' to Mr. Henry Yates Thompson, who had lately married his eldest daughter. Thenceforth the paper was wholly controlled by others. During the late seventies the pecuniary promise of the journal had not been sustained. It continued, however, to be characterised by good literary style, and to attract much literary ability, and it still justified its original aims of raising the literary standard of journalism

and of observing a severer code of journalistic morality
than had before been generally accepted. In 1870 Charles
Reade contributed characteristically polemical sketches
on social topics which were remunerated at an unusually
high rate. In 1871 Matthew Arnold contributed his
brilliantly sarcastic series of articles called ' Friendship's
Garland.' Richard Jefferies's 'The Gamekeeper at Home'
and others of the same writer's rural sketches appeared
serially from 1876 onwards. Almost all Jefferies's books
were published by Smith. At the same time other writers
on the paper gave him several opportunities of gratifying
his taste for fighting actions for libel. Dion Boucicault
in 1870, Hepworth Dixon in 1872, and Mr. W. S. Gilbert
in 1873, all crossed swords with him in the law courts on
account of what they deemed damaging reflections made
upon them in the ' Pall Mall Gazette ; ' but in each
instance the practical victory lay with Smith, and he was
much exhilarated by the encounters. At length, during
the crisis in Eastern Europe of 1876 and the following
years, the political tone of the paper became, under Mr.
Greenwood's guidance, unflinchingly Conservative. Smith,
although no strong partisan in politics, always inclined to
Liberalism ; and his sympathies with his paper in its existing condition waned, so that he parted from it without
much searching of heart.

To the end of his life Smith continued to give the
freest play to his instinct of hospitality. After 1872,
when he gave up his houses both at Hampstead and at
Brighton, he settled in South Kensington, where he
rented various residences from time to time up to 1891.
In that year he purchased the Duke of Somerset's mansion in Park Lane, which was his final London home.
From 1884 to 1897 he also had a residence near Weybridge. Of late years he usually spent the spring in the
Riviera, and on more than one occasion visited a German
watering-place in the summer. Wherever he lived he

welcomed no guests more frequently or with greater warmth than the authors and artists with whom he was professionally associated. His fund of entertaining reminiscence was unfailing, and his genial talk abounded in kindly reference to old friends and acquaintances. The regard in which he was held by those with whom he worked has been often indicated in the course of this memoir. It was conspicuously illustrated by the dying words of his lifelong friend Millais, who, when the power of speech had left him during his last illness in 1896, wrote on a slate the words, 'I should like to see George Smith, the kindest man and the best gentleman I have had to deal with.' The constancy which characterised his intimacies is well seen, too, in his relations with Mrs. Bryan Waller Procter. Thackeray had introduced him in comparatively early days to Procter and his family, and the daughter Adelaide, the well-known poetess, had excited his youthful admiration. When Procter was disabled by paralysis, and more especially after his death in 1874, Smith became Mrs. Procter's most valued friend and counsellor. He paid her a weekly visit, and thoroughly enjoyed her shrewd and pungent wit. She proved her confidence in him and her appreciation of the kindness he invariably showed her by presenting him with a volume of autograph letters that Thackeray had addressed to her and her husband, and finally she made him executor of her will. She died in 1888. To the last Smith's photograph always stood on her writing-table along with those of Robert Browning, James Russell Lowell, and Mr. Henry James, her three other closest allies. Another friend to whom Smith gave many proofs of attachment was Tom Hughes. Hughes was not one of Smith's authors. He had identified himself in early years too closely with the firm of Macmillan & Co. to connect himself with any other publisher. But he wrote occasionally for the 'Pall Mall Gazette;' he knew and liked Smith personally, and sought his counsel when the failure of his settlement at Rugby, Tennessee, was causing him great anxiety.

In 1878 Smith's mother died at the advanced age of eighty-one, having lived to see her son achieve fame and fortune. His eldest sister died two years later, and his only surviving sister, the youngest of the family, was left alone. Mainly in this sister's interest, Smith entered on a venture of a kind different from any he had yet essayed. He had made the acquaintance of Canon Barnett, vicar of St Jude's, who was persuading men of wealth to help in solving the housing question in the east end of London by purchasing some of the many barely habitable tenements that defaced the slums, by demolishing them, and by erecting on their sites blocks of model dwellings. It was one of the principles of Canon Barnett's treatment of the housing difficulty that the services of ladies should be enlisted as rent-collectors and managers of house property in poor districts. Under the advice of Canon Barnett, Smith, in 1880, raised a block of dwellings of a new and admirably sanitary type in George Yard in the very heart of Whitechapel. The block accommodated forty families, and the management was entrusted to his sister, who remained directress until her marriage, and was then succeeded by another lady. In carrying out this philanthropic scheme Smith proposed to work on business lines. He hoped to show in practice that capital might thus be invested at a fair profit, and thereby to induce others to follow his example. But the outlay somewhat exceeded the estimates, and, though a profit was returned, it was smaller than was anticipated. Smith, his wife, and his daughters took a warm interest in their tenants, whom for several winters they entertained at Toynbee Hall, and through many summers at their house at Weybridge. Many amusing stories used Smith to report of his conversation with his humble guests on these occasions.

VIII

In 1882 Smith resolved to embark on a new and final enterprise, which proved a fitting crown to his spirited career. In that year there first took shape in his mind the scheme of the 'Dictionary of National Biography,' with which his name must in future ages be chiefly identified. By his personal efforts, by his commercial instinct, by his masculine strength of mind and will, by his quickness of perception and by his industry, he had before 1882 built up a great fortune. But at no point of his life had it been congenial to his nature to restrict his activities solely to the accumulation of wealth. Now, in 1882, he set his mind upon making a munificent contribution to the literature of his country in the character not so much of a publisher seeking profitable investment for capital as of an enlightened man of wealth who desired at the close of his days to manifest his wish to serve his fellow countrymen and to merit their gratitude. On one or two public occasions he defined the motives that led him to the undertaking. At first he had contemplated producing a cyclopædia of universal biography ; but his friend Mr. Leslie Stephen, whom he took into his confidence, deemed the more limited form which the scheme assumed to be alone practicable. Smith was attracted by the notion of producing a book which would supply an acknowledged want in the literature of the country, and would compete with, or even surpass, works of a similar character which were being produced abroad. In foreign countries like encyclopædic work had been executed by means of Government subvention or under the auspices of State-aided literary academies. Smith's independence of temper was always strong, and he was inspirited by the knowledge that he was in a position to pursue single-handed an aim in behalf of which Government organisation had elsewhere been enlisted. It would be difficult in the history of

publishing to match the magnanimity of a publisher who
made up his mind to produce that kind of book for which
he had a personal liking, to involve himself in vast
expense, for the sake of an idea, in what he held to be the
public interest, without heeding considerations of profit or
loss. It was in the autumn of 1882 that, after long
consultation with Mr. Leslie Stephen, its first editor, the
'Dictionary of National Biography' was begun. Mr.
Stephen resigned the editorship of the ' Cornhill ' in order
to devote himself exclusively to the new enterprise. The
story of the progress of the publication has already been
narrated in the ' Statistical Account,' prefixed to the sixty-
third and last volume of the work, which appeared in July
1900. Here it need only be said that the literary result
did not disappoint Smith's expectations. As each quarterly
volume came with unbroken punctuality from the press he
perused it with an ever-growing admiration, and was
unsparing in his commendation and encouragement of
those who were engaged on the literary side of its production. In every detail of the work's general management
he took keen interest and played an active part in it from
first to last.

While the ' Dictionary ' was in progress many gratifying proofs were given Smith on the part of the public and
of the contributors, with whom his relations were uniformly cordial, of their appreciation of his patriotic
endeavour. After he had indulged his characteristically
hospitable instincts by entertaining them at his house in
Park Lane in 1892, they invited him to be their guest in
1894 at the Westminster Palace Hotel. Smith, in returning thanks, expressed doubt whether a publisher had ever
before been entertained by a distinguished company of
authors. In 1895 the university of Oxford conferred on
him the honorary degree of M.A. Some two years later,
on July 8, 1897, Smith acted as host to the whole body of
writers and some distinguished strangers at the Hôtel

Métropole, and six days afterwards, on July 14, 1897, at a
meeting of the second International Library Conference at
the Council Chamber in the Guildhall, a congratulatory
resolution was, on the motion of the late Dr. Justin
Winsor, librarian of Harvard, unanimously voted to him
' for carrying forward so stupendous a work.' The vote
was carried amid a scene of stirring enthusiasm. Smith
then said that during a busy life of more than fifty years
no work had afforded him so much interest and satisfaction as that connected with the ' Dictionary.' In May
1900, in view of the completion of the great undertaking,
King Edward VII. (then Prince of Wales) honoured with
his presence a small dinner party given to congratulate
Smith upon the auspicious event. Finally, on June 30,
1900, the Lord Mayor of London invited him and the
editors to a brilliant banquet at the Mansion House, which
was attended by men of the highest distinction in literature and public life. Mr. John Morley, in proposing the
chief toast, remarked that it was impossible to say too
much of the public spirit, the munificence, and the clear
and persistent way in which Smith had carried out the
great enterprise. He had not merely inspired a famous
literary achievement, but had done an act of good citizen-
ship of no ordinary quality or magnitude.

After 1890 Smith's active direction of affairs at
Waterloo Place, except in regard to the ' Dictionary of
National Biography,' somewhat diminished. From 1881
to 1890 his elder son, George Murray Smith, had joined
him in the publishing business; in 1890 his younger son,
Alexander Murray Smith, came in; and at the end of 1894
Reginald John Smith, K.C., who had shortly before married
Smith's youngest daughter, entered the firm. After 1894
Smith left the main control of the business in the hands
of his son, Alexander Murray Smith, and of his son-in-law,
Reginald John Smith, of whom the former retired from

active partnership early in 1899. Smith still retained the 'Dictionary' as his personal property, and until his death his advice and the results of his experience were placed freely and constantly at the disposal of his partners His interest in the fortunes of the firm was unabated to the end, and he even played anew in his last days his former rôle of adviser in the editorial conduct of the 'Cornhill Magazine.' The latest writer of repute and popularity, whose association with Smith, Elder, & Co. was directly due to himself, was Mrs. Humphry Ward, the niece of his old friend Matthew Arnold. In May 1886 she asked him to undertake the publication of her novel 'Robert Elsmere.' This he readily agreed to do, purchasing the right to issue fifteen hundred copies. It appeared in three volumes early in 1888. The work was triumphantly received, and it proved the first of a long succession of novels from the same pen which fully maintained the tradition of the publishing house in its relations with fiction. Smith followed with great sympathy Mrs. Ward's progress in popular opinion, and the cordiality that subsisted in her case, both privately and professionally, between author and publisher recalled the most agreeable experiences of earlier periods of his long career. He paid Mrs. Ward for her later work larger sums than any other novelist received from him, and in 1892, on the issue of 'David Grieve,' which followed 'Robert Elsmere,' he made princely terms for her with publishers in America.

In the summer of 1899, when Dr. Fitchett, the Australian writer, was on a visit to this country, he persuaded Smith to give him an opportunity of recording some of his many interesting reminiscences. The notes made by Dr. Fitchett largely deal with the early life, but Smith neither completed nor revised them, and they are not in a shape that permits of publication. Fragments of them formed the basis of four articles which he contributed to the 'Cornhill Magazine' in 1900-1.[1]

Although in early days the doctors credited Smith with a dangerous weakness of the heart and he suffered occasional illness, he habitually enjoyed good health till near the end of his life. He was tall and of a well-knit figure, retaining to an advanced age the bodily vigour and activity which distinguished him in youth. He always attributed his robustness in mature years to the constancy of his devotion to his favourite exercise of riding. After 1895 he suffered from a troublesome ailment which he bore with great courage and cheerfulness, but it was not till the beginning of 1901 that serious alarm was felt. An operation became necessary and was successfully performed on January 11, 1901, at his house in Park Lane. He failed, however, to recover strength; but, believing that his convalescence might be hastened by country air, he was at his own request removed in March to St. George's Hill, Byfleet, near Weybridge, a house which he had rented for a few months. After his arrival there he gradually sank, and he died on April 6. He was buried on the 11th in the churchyard at Byfleet. The progress of the supplemental volumes of the 'Dictionary,' which were then in course of preparation, was constantly in his mind during his last weeks of life, and the wishes that he expressed concerning them have been carried out. He bequeathed by will the 'Dictionary of National Biography' to his wife, who had throughout their married life been closely identified with all his undertakings, and was intimately associated with every interest of his varied career.

Smith was survived by his wife and all his children. His elder son, George Murray Smith, married in 1885

---

[1] The articles were 'In the Early Forties,' November 1900 ; 'Charlotte Brontë,' December 1900 ; 'Our Birth and Parentage,' January 1901 ; and 'Lawful Pleasures,' February 1901. He contemplated other papers of the like kind, but did not live to undertake them.

Ellen, youngest daughter of the first Lord Belper, and has issue three sons and a daughter. His younger son, Alexander Murray Smith, who was an active partner of the firm from 1890 to 1899, married in 1893 Emily Tennyson, daughter of Dr. Bradley, Dean of Westminster. His eldest daughter married in 1878 Henry Yates Thompson. His second daughter is Miss Ethel Murray Smith. His youngest daughter married in 1893 Reginald J. Smith, K.C., who joined the firm of Smith, Elder, and Co. at the end of 1894 and has been since 1899 sole active partner.

IX

In surveying the whole field of labour that Smith accomplished in his more than sixty years of adult life, one is impressed not merely by the amount of work that he achieved but by its exceptional variety. In him there were combined diverse ambitions and diverse abilities which are rarely found together in a single brain.

On the one hand he was a practical man of business, independent and masterful, richly endowed with financial instinct, most methodical, precise, and punctual in habits of mind and action. By natural temperament sanguine and cheerful, he was keen to entertain new suggestions, but the bold spirit of enterprise in him was controlled by a native prudence. In negotiation he was resolute yet cautious, and, scorning the pettiness of diplomacy, he was always alert to challenge in open fight dishonesty or meanness on the part of those with whom he had to transact affairs. Most of his mercantile ventures proved brilliant successes ; very few of them went far astray. His triumphs caused in him natural elation, but his cool judgment never suffered him to delude himself long with false hopes, and when defeat was unmistakable he faced it courageously and without repining. Although he was impatient of stupidity or carelessness, he was never a harsh taskmaster. He was, indeed, scrupulously just

F

and considerate in his dealings with those who worked
capably and loyally for him, and, being a sound judge of
men, seldom had grounds for regretting the bestowal of
his confidence.

These valuable characteristics account for only a part
of the interest attaching to Smith's career. They fail to
explain why he should have been for half a century not
merely one of the chief influences in the country which
helped literature and art conspicuously to flourish, but the
intimate friend, counsellor, and social ally of most of the
men and women who made the lasting literature and art of
his time. It would not be accurate to describe him as a
man of great imagination, or one possessed of literary or
artistic scholarship ; but it is bare truth to assert that his
masculine mind and temper were coloured by an intuitive
sympathy with the workings of the imagination in others ;
by a gift for distinguishing almost at a glance a good
piece of literature or art from a bad ; by an innate respect
for those who pursued intellectual and imaginative ideals
rather than mere worldly prosperity.

No doubt his love for his labours as a publisher was
partly due to the scope it gave to his speculative pro-
pensities, but it was due in a far larger degree to the
opportunities it offered him of cultivating the intimacy of
those whose attitude to life he whole-heartedly admired.
He realised the sensitiveness of men and women of
genius, and there were occasions on which he found himself unequal to the strain it imposed on him in his
business dealings ; but it was his ambition, as far as
was practicable, to conciliate it, and it was rarely that he
failed. He was never really dependent on the profits of
publishing, and, although he naturally engaged in it on
strict business principles, he knew how to harmonise such
principles with a liberal indulgence of the generous
impulses which wholly governed his private and domestic
life. His latest enterprise of the ' Dictionary of National

Biography' was a fitting embodiment of that native magnanimity which was the mainstay of his character, and gave its varied manifestations substantial unity.

[This memoir is partly based on the memoranda, recorded by Dr. Fitchett in 1899, to which reference has already been made (p. 63), and on the four articles respecting his early life which Smith contributed to the *Cornhill Magazine* November 1900 to February 1901. Valuable information has also been placed at the writer's disposal by Mrs. George M. Smith and Mrs. Yates Thompson, who have made many important suggestions. Numerous dates have been ascertained or confirmed by an examination of the account-books of Smith, Elder, & Co. Mention has already been made of Mrs. Gaskell's *Life of Charlotte Brontë*, Anthony Trollope's *Autobiography*, Mr. Leslie Stephen's *Life* of his brother Fitzjames, Matthew Arnold's *Letters* (ed. G. W. E. Russell), and other memoirs of authors in which reference is made to Smith. Mr. Leslie Stephen contributed an appreciative sketch 'In Memoriam' to the *Cornhill Magazine* for May 1901, and a memoir appeared in the *Times* of April 8, 1901. Thanks are due to Mr. C. R. Rivington, clerk of the Stationers' Company, for extracts from the Stationers' Company's Registers bearing on the firm's early history.]

SOME PAGES OF AUTOBIOGRAPHY

George Smith.

From the posthumous picture painted by
the Hon. John Collier in 1901.

I

IN THE EARLY FORTIES

Reprinted from the 'Cornhill Magazine,' November 1900

THOUGH it has often been suggested to me by friends who have been interested in my recollections of people I have known that I should put on record some of the incidents of a long and busy life, I doubt whether I should have taken up my pen, had it not been for the friendly pressure put on me by a distinguished man of letters from Australia who was recently on a visit to this country. It is chiefly at his instance that I have made up my mind to attempt a few jottings of my remembrances, beginning with very early days.

There are generally but few incidents, and these often only of trivial importance, that rest in one's memory after some sixty years ; but trivial as these incidents may have been in my experience, they brought me into contact with people and events which after so long a period of time may have a certain interest for the present generation.

Sixty years ago the business of Smith, Elder, & Co. was carried on at 65 Cornhill. It consisted chiefly of an export trade to India and our colonies. There was also a small publishing business, occasionally involving a certain amount of enterprise.

A recent festival in honour of the centenary of Lieutenant Waghorn's birth has brought to my mind incidents of my boyhood relating to that pioneer of the Overland Route to India, of whom I have a vivid remembrance.

At that time the long route round the Cape, occupying three or four months, was the only means of communication with India, and Waghorn's scheme for a shorter route across the Isthmus of Suez and through the Red Sea was eagerly welcomed by the commercial world. The English Government was chilly, if not indifferent, and private enterprise was left to demonstrate both the speed and the practicability of the new route. A number of merchants interested in the Eastern trade joined to bear the cost of some experimental trips by Waghorn. Letters to be sent to India in Waghorn's charge were brought to us to be stamped for express to Marseilles, where they were received by Waghorn and carried by him to Bombay. From Bombay in turn a packet of letters was brought by Waghorn to England.

I was eager, boy-like, to take part in this contest with time and space; my ambition was to ride one of the expresses between Paris and Marseilles, and I remember a fit of sulks which lasted for more than a week because my father refused his consent to this performance.

Waghorn, as I have said, received in Bombay a number of letters addressed to the various firms interested in the enterprise, and brought them *via* the Red Sea and Suez to London, thus showing by how many days he could beat the Cape route. The cost of this trip was distributed over the number of letters he carried, and charged as postage. The postage on the early Overland letters under this scheme was naturally alarming in scale; I can even now remember my father's face when he opened a letter brought by Waghorn, and containing a duplicate draft for 3*l*. or 4*l*., the postage for which was assessed at something like 25*l*. !

My father's firm acted as Waghorn's agents. All letters were brought to 65 Cornhill and posted thence. We youngsters used to think the receipt and stamping of these letters, for which we had an office at the back of

the shop, great fun ; it was like 'playing at post-office.'
Waghorn was a sailor-like man, short and broad, excitable
in a high degree, and of tremendous energy. He really
did a very great thing : he opened a new and shorter
route of intercourse between the East and the West ; but
the greatness of his feat was never properly recognised or
rewarded. He had an unfortunate gift for quarrelling
with people ; his energy was unqualified by tact ; his
temper was explosive. On one occasion I went into my
little room and found its floor strewn with fragments of
paper ; it was a copy of the 'Times' which contained an
article which did not please Waghorn, and he had
expressed his sentiments by furiously tearing the paper
into the tiniest fragments. More than once Waghorn
arrived at 65 Cornhill in the early morning when I was
the only member of the staff present. On one occasion
he arrived, travel-stained and dirty : he had just landed ;
and without a word of greeting he shouted, 'Have you
any one here who can run ?' I called in a ticket-porter
from the street : Waghorn inquired if he could run.
'Yes, sir,' said the porter, 'if I am paid for it.' Waghorn
handed him a packet and told him to run with it to the
Foreign Office. The ticket-porter was stout and scant of
breath ; running for him was a lost art. Waghorn
watched the man waddling down Cornhill ; he burst out
with a seafaring expletive, not to be repeated here, ran
after the porter, seized him by the coat-tails, which he
rent halfway up his back, grasped the packet, rolled the
unfortunate porter into the gutter, and ran off himself
with the despatches to the Foreign Office. I had to pick
the astonished porter from the gutter and pay him handsomely for his damaged coat and outraged feelings in
order to save Waghorn from a charge of assault.

Something of the spirit of modern trade, of its haste
and keenness, its eagerness to outrace not only all com-
petitors but time itself, was already visible in the opera-

tions of the firm. It seemed a great matter to them to
get periodicals and parcels off to India up to the latest
moment, and I can remember seeing a postchaise standing at the door of the shop in Cornhill to take parcels of
the 'Quarterly' or 'Edinburgh Review,' I forget which,
off to Deal to catch a fast ship there. It must, I suppose,
have contained some article of special interest to the
Indian public, but it was an expensive way of sending a
magazine, and could only 'pay' in the sense that getting
the Review to India before any other agent won for the
firm a reputation for energy and enterprise.

I recall another instance of these same characteristics.
The porter at the East India House, named Toole, used
to be sent to Gravesend with the latest despatches from
the India Office. He was a magnificent fellow, with a
splendid red livery—who, out of office hours, was widely
known as the best toast-master of his time ; his son, Mr.
John Lawrence Toole, is the genial actor who has
delighted several generations of playgoers. Some arrangement was come to with this gorgeous being, and he used
to carry, in addition to his despatches, packages of magazines and books for Smith, Elder, & Co.

As to my early attempts as a publisher, they began
when I was about nineteen years of age. I had then no
responsible position in the firm, but the business instinct
was slowly awaking in me. I was shrewd enough to see
that no steady policy was pursued in the publishing
department. If a book made a success, then for a time
almost everything that offered itself was accepted ; this
naturally produced a harvest of disasters ; then for a while
nothing at all was published. Various efforts were made
to improve the management of the publishing department,
to which the members of the firm were unable to give
much personal attention. A Mr. Folthorp, who afterwards had a large Library at Brighton, was engaged as
manager, but with little success ; a Mr. Reid followed

him, and he also was a failure. I had often discussed the matter with my mother, who had a keen and businesslike intelligence ; I was eager to assume a responsible position in the business, and on the deposition of Mr. Reid, my mother persuaded my father, who in turn persuaded his partners, to put me in charge of the publishing department. I was to have the modest sum of 1,500l. at my absolute disposal. I stipulated that I was not to be questioned or interfered with in any way as to its use ; with this sum I was to make what publishing ventures I pleased. Behold me then, a youth not yet twenty, searching the horizon for authors whose literary bantlings I might introduce to an admiring and, as I fondly hoped, purchasing world.

My first venture was the publication of R. H. Horne's —'Orion' Horne's—'New Spirit of the Age'—a series of essays on well-known living writers. I doubt whether any publisher has ever been so much interested in a book as I was in these two volumes. It was, from the publisher's point of view, my first-born. I have since had publishing and commerical ventures involving comparatively very large sums, but not one has ever given me such anxious care as these volumes. I read every line of the book, first in manuscript and then in proof ; I poured upon the unfortunate author all sorts of youthful criticisms and suggestions. I had sleepless nights over the book. At last we came to a deadlock. The book included an article on Colonel Perronet Thompson, a leading and very advanced politician of the day. Horne's study of Thompson was enthusiastic ; his views were not in the least likely to commend themselves to the book-buying public of that time. I felt very much as I imagine the editor of the 'Quarterly Review' would feel if invited to accept a eulogium, say, of Mr. John Burns by Mr. Keir Hardie. I remonstrated with Horne, who replied that Thompson was a man of sufficient distinction to find a place in the volume, and was a man with a future. A long correspondence followed, dreadfully in earnest on my side, but Horne was firm. At length I went to Horne's residence at Kentish Town to endeavour to settle the matter in person. I have still a vivid remembrance of the interview which followed, and had a sufficient sense of humour to appreciate its absurdity even in my anxious condition of mind. I argued the matter with great earnestness, employing all the eloquent phrases I had invented during my ride to Kentish Town on the outside of an omnibus. Horne at last said, ' My dear young friend, you are rather excited. Let us have a little music.' He fetched his guitar and played to me for half an hour; he then asked if my views were still the same. He found they had resisted even the strains of his guitar. Then Horne's good-nature came to my aid. He opened his bookcase, beckoned to me with the gesture of a tragic actor to approach. He took up the offending manuscript, written on brief-paper, held one corner in his hand, and motioned to me with the utmost solemnity to take the other corner. We then proceeded in funereal silence, keeping step as in a stage procession, to the fireplace, when Horne looked me in the face with a tragic expression, and said, ' Throw.' We threw; the offending manuscript dropped into the flames; Horne heaved a deep sigh, and I shook him warmly by the hand and departed much relieved. Any one who remembers the quaint and picturesque personality of the author of ' Orion ' will be able to appreciate this scene.

Thackeray reviewed Horne's book in the ' Morning Chronicle,' and on the whole favourably, though he sadly hurt Horne's feelings by in effect calling him a Cockney, which to Horne seemed the sum of all discredit. The droll little man came to Cornhill with the preface to a new edition in which he proposed to overwhelm his critics, including Thackeray. We adjourned to the ' Woolpack,'

a tavern in St. Peter's Alley, Cornhill, where I generally
had my lunch, and there in a quiet room upstairs the
preface was discussed. I remember how vain I felt at
having suggested an expression about ' the scorching glare
of the Bay of Mexico, or the thunders of the Gulf of
Florida,' which Horne accepted with acclamation as a
substitute for some tamer phrase he had used.

Horne was a kindly, clever little man, but he was an
oddity. He published the first three editions of ' Orion '
at a farthing a copy ; the price of the fourth edition was,
I believe, a shilling, and that of the fifth, half-a-crown.
His quaintness took many turns. Among other eccentric
opinions cherished by him was one that Shylock was a
misunderstood character to whom justice had never been
done. Shylock, Horne contended, only asked what was
his due. Shakespeare's conception of the character, he
held, had never been really placed before the public, and
he determined to remedy this ancient injustice and repair
the wrong done to Shylock by representing him as, in his
opinion, he ought to be represented on the stage. The
' Merchant of Venice ' was played at a theatre in the
Tottenham Court Road, and Horne, the only amateur in
the company, took the part of Shylock. The house was
filled with his friends eager to study the new Shylock,
and I can remember nothing more comic than Horne's
rendering of the character. We bit our lips, we held our
handkerchiefs to our mouths, we used every artifice at our
command to conceal our laughter. We were fairly
successful until Horne, with an air of much dignity,
sharpened his knife on the floor of the stage ; then we
exploded, and Horne's efforts to give to the world a white-
washed Shylock came to an abrupt end.

Horne had undoubtedly a strain of genius, but it was
linked to a most uncertain judgment, and was often
qualified by a plentiful lack of common sense. He once
submitted to me the manuscript of a most extraordinary

novel. It was wonderfully clever, but, from a publisher's point of view, was quite impossible. It was written to sustain the proposition that every man and every woman had a preordained and natural affinity for some other particular man or woman, and this theory was illustrated from a rather coarse and physical point of view which certainly offended severe taste. The characters of the novel were extraordinary; one of the most extraordinary was a philanthropist impressed with the idea that the world was overpopulated and anxious on grounds of purest benevolence to remedy the mistake by murdering as many people as he could. His numerous murders were transacted in a very odd fashion. He had his own leg cut off below the knee, and a wooden leg fitted on in its stead. This innocent-looking wooden leg was really a disguised rifle or air-gun. Every now and again a corpse was found with a bullet hole in it; the neighbourhood was searched, but no trace of the murderer could be found. At last it occurred to the magistrate that there was always an old man with a wooden leg somewhere in the neighbourhood when one of these murders was committed. This led to the detection of the eccentric philanthropist, who, in spite of the benevolence of his motives, was broken by unsympathetic legal authorities on the wheel. This curious philanthropist used to engage his intended victim in conversation, cock his wooden leg in an apparently careless fashion over the other knee, and suddenly shoot his unsuspecting interlocutor dead. And the writer of this extravagant novel was the author of 'Orion'! I refused, much to Horne's disgust, to publish the work, and it never, I believe, found a publisher.

My next publishing venture brought me into relations with Leigh Hunt, and did so in rather a strange way. I went to Peckham to dine with Thomas Powell, who as well as being a confidential clerk in the counting-house of two brothers who were wealthy merchants in the City

dabbled in literature. The merchants were supposed to
have suggested to Charles Dickens the Cheeryble Brothers
in 'Nicholas Nickleby.' Powell afterwards went to the
United States and contributed articles of a very personal
character to the New York newspapers about English
men of letters. While I waited in Powell's little drawing-
room for a few minutes before dinner, I took up a neatly
written manuscript which was lying on the table, and was
reading it when my host entered the room. 'Ah,' he said
'that doesn't look worth 40l., does it?   I advance 40l. to
Leigh Hunt on the security of that manuscript, and I
shall never see my money again.'   When I was leaving I
asked Powell to let me take the manuscript with me.   I
finished reading it before I went to sleep that night, and
next day I asked Powell if he would let me have the
manuscript if I paid him the 40l. He readily assented,
and having got from him Leigh Hunt's address, I went off
to him in Edwardes Square, Kensington, explained the
circumstances under which the manuscript had come into
my possession, and asked whether, if I paid him an additional 60l., I might have the copyright.   'You young
prince!' cried Leigh Hunt, in a tone of something like
rapture, and the transaction was promptly concluded. The
work was 'Imagination and Fancy.' It was succeeded by
'Wit and Humour' and other books, all of which were
successful, and the introduction was the foundation of a
friendship with Leigh Hunt and the members of his
family which was very delightful to me.

Leigh Hunt was of tall stature, with sallow, not to say
yellow, complexion. His mouth lacked refinement and
firmness, but he had large expressive eyes. His manner,
however, had such fascination that, after he had spoken
for five minutes, one forgot how he looked. He wrote
the most charming letters, perfect alike in both form and
spirit. I particularly enjoyed the simple old-fashioned
suppers to which he frequently invited me. His daughter

played and sang to us, and Leigh Hunt told us the most delightful stories of his Italian travels, and of Shelley and Byron (whom he always called ' Birron '). I lived on the north side of the park, and I remember I used to get over the palings to cross Kensington Gardens, and thus shorten the distance home ; the palings of those days were easily negotiated by an active young man.

Business was by no means Leigh Hunt's strong point. In this respect, but no otherwise, he may have suggested Skimpole to Charles Dickens. On one of my visits I found him trying to puzzle out the abstruse question of how he should deduct some such sum as thirteen shillings and ninepence from a sovereign. On another occasion I had to pay him a sum of money, 100*l*. or 200*l*., and I wrote him a cheque for the amount. ' Well,' he said, ' what am I to do with this little bit of paper ? ' I told him that if he presented it at the bank they would pay him cash for it, but I added, ' I will save you that trouble.' I sent to the bank and cashed the cheque for him. He took the notes away carefully enclosed in an envelope. Two days afterward Leigh Hunt came in a state of great agitation to tell me that his wife had burned them. He had thrown the envelope with the bank-notes inside carelessly down and his wife had flung it into the fire. Leigh Hunt's agitation while on his way to bring this news had not prevented him from purchasing on the road a little statuette of Psyche which he carried, without any paper round it, in his hand. I told him I thought something might be done in the matter ; I sent to the bankers and got the numbers of the notes, and then in company with Leigh Hunt went off to the Bank of England. I explained our business and we were shown into a room where three old gentlemen were sitting at tables. They kept us waiting some time, and Leigh Hunt, who had meantime been staring all round the room, at last got up, walked up to one of the staid officials, and addressing him said in

wondering tones, 'And this is the Bank of England! And
do you sit here all day, and never see the green woods and
the trees and flowers and the charming country?' Then
in tones of remonstrance he demanded, 'Are you contented
with such a life?' All this time he was holding the little
naked Pysche in one hand, and with his long hair and
flashing eyes made a surprising figure. I fancy I can still
see the astonished faces of the three officials; they would
have made a most delightful picture. I said 'Come
away, Mr. Hunt; these gentlemen are very busy.' I
succeeded in carrying Leigh Hunt off, and after entering
into certain formalities, we were told that the value of the
notes would be paid in twelve months. I gave Leigh
Hunt the money at once, and he went away rejoicing.

On the whole my first modest experiences in publishing were successful, and brought me into pleasant
social relations with several authors. I remember I was
very indignant that the firm would not allow me to add
the profits of my ventures to the original sum which
formed my publishing capital. I had reckoned on
increasing that capital by the profits I made until I could
undertake really large transactions; but this expectation
was disappointed, and my yearly profits melted into the
general balance sheet of the firm.

G

II

CHARLOTTE BRONTË

Reprinted from the ' Cornhill Magazine,' December 1900

THE ten years from 1840 to 1850 were a very eventful decade to me. In 1844 my father fell into ill health, and went to live at Box Hill near Dorking, where he died in August 1846. Mr. Elder had never taken a leading part in the business, and when my father's health broke down the general management to a great extent fell on me. At this time I was twenty years of age. In the year 1845 we had to face the fact that my father's condition was hopeless, and he retired from the firm. Mr. Elder deciding to retire at the same time, a new partnership was constituted by the remaining partner (whose name I prefer not to mention) and myself. The partnership lasted only about two years, after which time I was under the painful necessity of dissolving it. The entire control of the business now fell upon my rather youthful shoulders. My condition was a very anxious one : nearly every penny my father possessed had been invested in the business ; the provision for my mother and my young brothers and sisters was absolutely dependent on its success ; and although the business was a profitable one, I had the gravest reasons for anxiety as to its financial position, which had been cruelly undermined. It will be seen that the situation was one to bring out whatever there was in me, and I worked with all the intensity and zeal of which I was capable. The work I got through may be described as enormous. In addition to my previous responsibilities, I had to take in hand the Indian and Colonial correspondence, of which my partner had previously been in charge. This work was, of course, more difficult for me at first, as the details of it were new, but I quickly mastered it. I must in those days have had great powers of endurance ; the correspondence was heavy, the letters were often both very long and very important ; I used to dictate to a clerk while two others were occupied in copying. It was a common thing for me and many of the clerks to work until three or four o'clock in the morning, and occasionally, when there was but a short interval between the arrival and departure of the Indian mails, I used to start work at nine o'clock of one morning, and neither leave my room nor cease dictating until seven o'clock the next evening, when the mail was despatched. During these thirty-two hours of continuous work I was supported by mutton-chops and green tea at stated intervals. I believe I maintained my health by active exercise on foot and horseback, and by being able after these excessive stretches of work to sleep soundly for many hours ; on these occasions I generally got to bed at about eleven, and slept till three or four o'clock the next afternoon.

Happily for me my mother removed to London shortly after my father's death, and I had the advantage of her daily support and sympathy. Naturally the hard work was not the worst for me ; the continuous anxiety and sense of responsibility from which I had to suffer were even more crushing. Had it not been that I had in my mother a woman of the most indomitable courage, I do not believe that I could have sustained the combined stress of anxiety and work. My mother's cheerful spirit never forsook her : in looking back I can see that she devoted herself to sustaining my courage ; she even made fun of our perilous position. On one Sunday, when I was unusually depressed, she took me for a walk in Kensington Gardens; a more wretched creature than I felt, and I suppose looked, when we started for our walk could hardly be imagined, but my mother had evidently set her heart on cheering me. She had some gift of mimicry, and she drew such a humorous picture of the result of our utter ruin, when she expressed her intention, if the worst came, of having a Berlin wool shop in the Edgware Road, and so admirably mimicked one of my sisters—who was regarded in the family as having rather a taste for display—serving behind the counter, that I could not restrain my laughter, and returned home in a different and more hopeful condition of mind.

At this time I was unable to give much attention to the publishing business, but the firm produced some books of importance, and if these unpretentious jottings are found interesting by the readers of the 'Cornhill Magazine,' I may possibly ask the editor to give his consideration to a few of my reminiscences of their authors and of other writers whom I have known subsequently. Meanwhile I propose to devote the present paper to some recollections of a writer whose personality, as well as, or even more than, her literary gifts, was always interesting to me.

In July 1847 a parcel containing a MS. reached our office addressed to the firm, but bearing also the scored-out addresses of three or four other publishing houses; showing that the parcel had been previously submitted to other publishers. This was not calculated to prepossess us in favour of the MS. It was clear that we were offered what had been already rejected elsewhere.

The parcel contained the MS. of 'The Professor,' by 'Currer Bell,' a book which was published after Charlotte Brontë's death. Mr. Williams, the 'reader' to the firm, read the MS., and said that it evinced great literary power, but he had doubts as to its being successful as a publication. We decided that he should write to 'Currer Bell' a letter of appreciative criticism declining the work, but expressing an opinion that he could produce a book which would command success. Before, however, our letter was despatched, there came a letter from 'Currer Bell' containing a postage-stamp for our reply, it having been hinted to the writer by 'an experienced friend' that publishers often refrained from answering communications unless a postage-stamp was furnished for the purpose! Charlotte Brontë herself has described the effect our letter had on her :

As a forlorn hope, he tried one publishing house more. Ere long, in a much shorter space than that on which experience had taught him to calculate, there came a letter, which he opened in the dreary anticipation of finding two hard hopeless lines, intimating that 'Messrs. Smith, Elder, & Co. were not disposed to publish the MS.,' and, instead, he took out of the envelope a letter of two pages. He read it trembling. It declined, indeed, to publish that tale for business reasons, but it discussed its merits and demerits so courteously, so considerately, in a spirit so rational, with a discrimination so enlightened, that this very refusal cheered the author better than a vulgarly expressed acceptance would have done. It was added, that a work in three volumes would meet with careful attention.

The writer of this letter was, as I have said, Mr. W. Smith Williams, and his name appears so frequently in all accounts of the Brontë family that a brief mention of his relations with Smith, Elder, & Co. may be interesting.

When I first came into control of the business I felt the necessity of getting efficient assistance in the publishing department. A happy accident gave me the man I sought. The accounts of the firm had fallen into some confusion in consequence of my father's illness. Mr. Elder, who, on my father's breakdown, had taken charge of them, was but a poor accountant. Among the first tasks to which I devoted myself was that of bringing the

accounts into order.   An account with the lithographers
who had printed the illustrations for Darwin's ' Zoology
of the Voyage of H.M.S. " Beagle," ' and for other books
of smaller magnitude, was in an almost hopeless state of
confusion.   It had not been balanced for years, sums
having being paid ' on account' from time to time.

I went to see the bookkeeper of the firm of lithographers—Mr. W Smith Williams—taking with me a
bundle of accounts with a view to getting them arranged
in proper form.   Mr. Williams's gifts as a bookkeeper I
soon found were of a most primitive character.   I asked
him how he had struck his numerous balances, remarking
that we had no corresponding balances in our books.
' Oh ! ' said Mr. Williams, ' those are the bottoms of the
pages in our ledger ; I always strike a balance at the
bottom of a page to avoid the necessity of carrying over
the figures on both sides.'   I had a good many interviews
with Mr. Williams, and if he was not a good bookkeeper,
he was a most agreeable and most intelligent man, a man
with literary gifts wasted in uncongenial work.   My
sympathy was excited by seeing one of so much ability
occupied with work which he did ill, and which was
distasteful to him ; and by noticing the overbearing
manner in which he was treated by the junior member of
the firm which employed him.   Mr. Williams confided to
me that, by way of relief from his bookkeeping efforts, he
contributed reviews and other articles to the ' Spectator,'
then making its high position under the able editorship
of Mr. Rintoul.   Mr. Williams used also to write theatrical
criticisms for the ' Spectator,' but found himself hampered
a good deal, he said, by the chilly temperament of his
editor, Mr. Rintoul, who used to say, in the most im-
pressive manner, ' The " Spectator " is *not* enthusiastic,
and must not be ' !

I fancied I had discovered the man who could help
me in my publishing business.   I invited Mr. Williams

to tea at my lodgings in Regent Street, and after tea I said to him, ' Rightly or wrongly, I do not think you like your present occupation ? ' ' I *hate* it,' said Mr. Williams with fervour. This reply made clear sailing for me, and before he left my room we had arranged that he should come to Cornhill as my literary assistant, and general manager of the publishing department. It was for both of us a happy arrangement. Mr. Williams remained with me until his advancing years obliged him to retire from active work. He was loyal, diligent, of shrewd literary judgment and pleasant manners, and proved a most valuable assistant ; and his relations with me and my family were always of the most cordial description.

In reply to Mr. Williams's letter came a brief note from ' Currer Bell,' expressing grateful appreciation of the attention which had been given to the MS., and saying that the author was on the point of finishing another book, which would be sent to us as soon as completed.

The second MS. was ' Jane Eyre.' Here again ' Currer Bell's ' suspicion as to the excessive parsimony of London publishers in regard to postage-stamps found expression in the letter accompanying the MS. She wrote :

I find I cannot prepay the carriage of the parcel, as money for that purpose is not received at the small station where it is left. If, when you acknowledge the receipt of the MS., you would have the goodness to mention the amount charged on delivery, I will immediately transmit it in postage-stamps.

The MS. of ' Jane Eyre ' was read by Mr. Williams in due course. He brought it to me on a Saturday, and said that he would like me to read it. There were no Saturday half-holidays in those days, and, as was usual, I did not reach home until late. I had made an appointment with a friend for Sunday morning ; I was to meet him about twelve o'clock, at a place some two or three miles from our house, and ride with him into the country.

After breakfast on Sunday morning I took the MS. of 'Jane Eyre' to my little study, and began to read it The story quickly took me captive. Before twelve o'clock my horse came to the door, but I could not put the book down. I scribbled two or three lines to my friend, saying I was very sorry that circumstances had arisen to prevent my meeting him, sent the note off by my groom, and went on reading the MS. Presently the servant came to tell me that luncheon was ready; I asked him to bring me a sandwich and a glass of wine, and still went on with 'Jane Eyre.' Dinner came; for me the meal was a very hasty one, and before I went to bed that night I had finished reading the manuscript.

The next day we wrote to 'Currer Bell' accepting the book for publication. I need say nothing about the success which the book achieved, and the speculations as to whether it was written by a man or a woman. For my own part I never had much doubt on the subject of the writer's sex; but then I had the advantage over the general public of having the handwriting of the author before me. There were qualities of style, too, and turns of expression, which satisfied me that 'Currer Bell' was a woman, an opinion in which Mr. Williams concurred. We were bound, however, to respect the writer's anonymity, and our letters continued to be addressed to 'Currer Bell, Esq.' Her sisters were always referred to in the correspondence as 'Messrs. Ellis and Acton Bell.' The works of Ellis and Acton Bell had been published by a Mr. Newby, on terms which rather depleted the scanty purses of the authors. When we were about to publish 'Shirley'—the work which, in the summer of 1848, succeeded 'Jane Eyre'—we endeavoured to make an arrangement with an American publisher to sell him advance sheets of the book, in order to give him an advantage in regard to time over other American pub-lishers. There was, of course, no copyright with America in those days. We were met during the negotiations with our American correspondents by the statement that Mr. Newby had informed them that he was about to publish the next book by the author of 'Jane Eyre,' under her other *nom de plume* of Acton Bell—Currer, Ellis, and Acton Bell being in fact, according to him, one person. We wrote to 'Currer Bell' to say that we should be glad to be in a position to contradict the statement, adding at the same time we were quite sure Mr. Newby's assertion was untrue. Charlotte Brontë has related how the letter affected her. She was persuaded that her honour was impugned. 'With rapid decision,' says Mrs. Gaskell in her 'Life of Charlotte Brontë,' 'Charlotte and her sister Anne resolved that they should start for London that very day in order to prove their separate identity to Messrs. Smith, Elder, & Co.'

With what haste and energy the sisters plunged into what was, for them, a serious expedition, how they reached London at eight o'clock on a Saturday morning, took lodgings in the 'Chapter' coffee-house in Paternoster Row, and, after an agitated breakfast, set out on a pilgrimage to my office in Cornhill, is told at length in Mrs. Gaskell's 'Life of Charlotte Brontë.'

That particular Saturday morning I was at work in my room, when a clerk reported that two ladies wished to see me. I was very busy and sent out to ask their names. The clerk returned to say that the ladies declined to give their names, but wished to see me on a private matter. After a moment's hesitation I told him to show them in. I was in the midst of my correspondence, and my thoughts were far away from 'Currer Bell' and 'Jane Eyre.' Two rather quaintly dressed little ladies, pale-faced and anxious-looking, walked into my room ; one of them came forward and presented me with a letter addressed, in my own handwriting, to 'Currer Bell, Esq.' I noticed that the letter had been opened, and said, with some sharpness,

' Where did you get this from ? '   ' From the post-office,'
was the reply ; ' it was addressed to me.   We have both
come that you might have ocular proof that there are at
least two of us.'   This then was ' Currer Bell ' in person.
I need hardly say that I was at once keenly interested,
not to say excited.   Mr. Williams was called down and
introduced, and I began to plan all sorts of attentions to
our visitors.   I tried to persuade them to come and stay
at our house.   This they positively declined to do, but
they agreed that I should call with my sister and take
them to the Opera in the evening.   She has herself given
an account of her own and her sister Anne's sensations
on that occasion : how they dressed for the Opera in their
plain, high-necked dresses :

> Fine ladies and gentlemen glanced at us, as we stood by
> the box-door, which was not yet opened, with a slight graceful
> superciliousness, quite warranted by the circumstances.   Still
> I felt pleasurably excited in spite of headache, sickness, and
> conscious clownishness ; and I saw Anne was calm and
> gentle, which she always is.   The performance was Rossini's
> *Barber of Seville*—very brilliant, though I fancy there are
> things I should like better.   We got home after one o'clock.
> We had never been in bed the night before ; had been in
> constant excitement for twenty-four hours ; you may imagine
> we were tired.

My mother called upon them the next day.   The
sisters, after barely three days in London, returned to
Haworth.   In what condition of mind and body those
few days left them is graphically told by Charlotte Brontë
herself :

> On Tuesday morning we left London, laden with books Mr.
> Smith had given us, and got safely home.   A more jaded
> wretch than I looked, it would be difficult to conceive.   I was
> thin when I went, but I was meagre indeed when I returned,
> my face looking grey and very old, with strange deep lines
> ploughed in it—my eyes stared unnaturally.   I was weak and
> yet restless.

This is the only occasion on which I saw Anne Brontë. She was a gentle, quiet, rather subdued person, by no means pretty, yet of a pleasing appearance. Her manner was curiously expressive of a wish for protection and encouragement, a kind of constant appeal which invited sympathy.

I must confess that my first impression of Charlotte Brontë's personal appearance was that it was interesting rather than attractive. She was very small, and had a quaint old-fashioned look. Her head seemed too large for her body. She had fine eyes, but her face was marred by the shape of the mouth and by the complexion. There was but little feminine charm about her; and of this fact she herself was uneasily and perpetually conscious. It may seem strange that the possession of genius did not lift her above the weakness of an excessive anxiety about her personal appearance. But I believe that she would have given all her genius and her fame to have been beautiful. Perhaps few women ever existed more anxious to be pretty than she, or more angrily conscious of the circumstance that she was *not* pretty.

Charlotte Brontë stayed with us several times. The utmost was, of course, done to entertain and please her. We arranged for dinner-parties, at which artistic and literary notabilities, whom she wished to meet, were present. We took her to places which we thought would interest her—the 'Times' office, the General Post Office, the Bank of England, Newgate, Bedlam. At Newgate she rapidly fixed her attention on an individual prisoner. This was a poor girl with an interesting face, and an expression of the deepest misery. She had, I believe, killed her illegitimate child. Miss Brontë walked up to her, took her hand, and began to talk to her. She was, of course, quickly interrupted by the prison warder with the formula, 'Visitors are not allowed to speak to the prisoners.' Sir David Brewster took her round the Great

Exhibition, and made the visit a very interesting one to her. One thing which impressed her very much was the lighted rooms of the newspaper offices in Fleet Street and the Strand, as we drove home in the middle of the night from some City expedition.

On one occasion I took Miss Brontë to the Ladies' Gallery of the House of Commons. The Ladies' Gallery of those days was behind the Strangers' Gallery, and from it one could see the eyes of the ladies above, nothing more. I told Miss Brontë that if she felt tired and wished to go away, she had only to look at me—I should know by the expression of her eyes what she meant—and that I would come round for her. After a time I looked and looked. There were many eyes, they all seemed to be flashing signals to me, but much as I admired Miss Brontë's eyes I could not distinguish them from the others. I looked so earnestly from one pair of eyes to another that I am afraid that more than one lady must have regarded me as a rather impudent fellow. At length I went round and took my lady away. I expressed my hope that I did not keep her long waiting, and said something about the difficulty of getting out after I saw her signal. 'I made no signal,' she said. 'I did not wish to come away. Perhaps there were other signals from the Gallery.'

Miss Brontë and her father had a passionate admiration for the Duke of Wellington, and I took her to the Chapel Royal, St. James's, which he generally attended on Sunday, in order that she might see him. We followed him out of the Chapel, and I indulged Miss Brontë by so arranging our walk that she met him twice on his way to Apsley House. I also took her to a Friends' meeting-house in St. Martin's Court, Leicester Square. I am afraid this form of worship afforded her more amusement than edification.

We went together to a Dr. Browne, a phrenologist

who was then in vogue, using the names of Mr. and Miss Fraser. Here is Dr. Browne's estimate of the talents and disposition of Miss Brontë:

A PHRENOLOGICAL ESTIMATE OF THE TALENTS AND DISPOSITIONS OF A LADY.

Temperament for the most part nervous. Brain large, the anterior and superior parts remarkably salient. In her domestic relations this lady will be warm and affectionate. In the care of children she will evince judicious kindness, but she is not pleased at seeing them spoiled by over-indulgence. Her fondness for any particular locality would chiefly rest upon the associations connected with it. Her attachments are strong and enduring—indeed, this is a leading element of her character; she is rather circumspect, however, in the choice of her friends, and it is well that she is so, for she will seldom meet with persons whose dispositions approach the standard of excellence with which she can entirely sympathise. Her sense of truth and justice would be offended by any dereliction of duty, and she would in such cases express her disapprobation with warmth and energy; she would not, however, be precipitate in acting thus, and rather than live in a state of hostility with those she could wish to love she would depart from them, although the breaking-off of friendship would be to her a source of great unhappiness. The careless and unreflecting, whom she would labour to amend, might deem her punctilious and perhaps exacting; not considering that their amendment and not her own gratification prompted her to admonish. She is sensitive and is very anxious to succeed in her undertakings, but is not so sanguine as to the probability of success. She is occasionally inclined to take a gloomier view of things than perhaps the facts of the case justify; she should guard against the effect of this where her affection is engaged, for her sense of her own importance is moderate and not strong enough to steel her heart against disappointment; she has more firmness than self-reliance, and her sense of justice is of a very high order. She is deferential to the aged and those she deems worthy of respect, and possesses much devotional feeling, but dislikes fanaticism and is not given to a belief in supernatural things without questioning the probability of their existence.

Money is not her idol : she values it merely for its uses ; she would be liberal to the poor and compassionate to the afflicted, and when friendship calls for aid she would struggle even against her own interest to impart the required assistance—indeed, sympathy is a marked characteristic of this organisation.

Is fond of symmetry and proportion, and possesses a good perception of form, and is a good judge of colour. She is endowed with a keen perception of melody and rhythm. Her imitative powers are good, and the faculty which gives manual dexterity is well developed. These powers might have been cultivated with advantage. Is a fair calculator, and her sense of order and arrangement is remarkably good. Whatever this lady has to settle or arrange will be done with precision and taste.

She is endowed with an exalted sense of the beautiful and ideal, and longs for perfection. If not a poet her sentiments are poetical, or are at least imbued with that enthusiastic glow which is characteristic of poetical feeling. She is fond of dramatic literature and the drama, especially if it be combined with music.

In its intellectual development this head is very remarkable. The forehead is at once very large and well formed. It bears the stamp of deep thoughtfulness and comprehensive understanding. It is highly philosophical. It exhibits the presence of an intellect at once perspicacious and perspicuous. There is much critical sagacity and fertility in devising resources in situations of difficulty, much originality, with a tendency to speculate and generalise. Possibly this speculative bias may sometimes interfere with the practical efficiency of some of her projects. Yet since she has scarcely an adequate share of self-reliance, and is not sanguine as to the success of her plans, there is reason to suppose that she would attend more closely to particulars, and thereby present the unsatisfactory results of hasty generalisation. This lady possesses a fine organ of language, and can, if she has done her talents justice by exercise, express her sentiments with clearness, precision, and force—sufficiently eloquent but not verbose. In learning a language she would investigate its spirit and structure. The character of the German language would be well adapted to such an organisation. In analysing the motives of human conduct, this lady would display originality and power, but in her mode of investigating mental science she would naturally be imbued with a metaphysical bias; she would perhaps be sceptical as to the truth of Gale's doctrine. But the study of this doctrine, this new system of mental philosophy, would give additional strength to her excellent understanding by rendering it more practical, more attentive to particulars, and contribute to her happiness by imparting to her more correct notions of the dispositions of those whose acquaintance she may wish to cultivate.

T. P. BROWNE, M.D.

367 Strand, June 29, 1851.

Dr. Browne could not have had any idea whose head he was examining. A few days afterwards Mr. Richard Doyle, whom I used to see frequently, mentioned that a friend of his had examined the head of a lady, and was so much struck by the imaginative power she possessed that he should like to find out something about her. 'If he succeeds,' said Richard Doyle, 'I will tell you who she is ; for, if Dr. Browne is right, the lady ought to be worth your looking after.' The estimate of my own head was not so happy. From the frequent reference to it and to Mr. Fraser in Miss Brontë's letters to me I must have sent it to her, and I cannot find that I have kept a copy.

Her letters show that she enjoyed the recollection of these visits, and the society at our house; but my mother and sisters found her a somewhat difficult guest, and I am afraid she was never perfectly at her ease with them. Strangers used to say that they were afraid of her. She was very quiet and self-absorbed, and gave the impression that she was always engaged in observing and analysing the people she met. She was sometimes tempted to confide her analysis to the victim. Here is an extract from a letter which she wrote to myself :

I will tell you a thing to be noted often in your letters and almost always in your conversation, a psychological thing, and not a matter pertaining to style or intellect—I mean an under-current of quiet raillery, an inaudible laugh to yourself, a not unkindly, but somewhat subtle playing on your correspondent or companion for the time being—in short a sly touch of a Mephistopheles with the fiend extracted. In the present instance this speciality is perceptible only in the slightest degree, but it *is* there, and more or less you have it always. I by no means mention this as a *fault.* I merely tell you you have it, and I can make the accusation with comfortable impunity, guessing pretty surely that you are too busy just now to deny this or any other charge.

For my own part, I found her conversation most inter-esting; her quick and clear intelligence was delightful. When she became excited on any subject she was really eloquent, and it was a pleasure to listen to her.

On an occasion when I took her to dine with Mr. Thackeray the excitement with which Charlotte Brontë's visit was expected is portrayed by Miss Thackeray, who was then a mere child :

I can still see the scene quite plainly !—the hot summer evening, the open windows, the carriage driving to the door as we all sat silent and expectant ; my father, who rarely waited, waiting with us : our governess, my sister, and I all in a row, and prepared for the great event. We saw the carriage stop and out of it sprang the active, well-knit figure of young Mr. George Smith, who was bringing Miss Brontë to see our father. My father, who had been walking up and down the room, goes out into the hall to meet his guests, and then after a moment's delay the door opens wide, and the two gentlemen come in, leading a tiny, delicate, serious, little lady, pale, with fair straight hair, and steady eyes. She may be a little over thirty ; she is dressed in a little *barège* dress with a pattern of faint green moss. She enters in mittens, in silence, in seriousness ; our hearts are beating with wild excitement.

Charlotte Brontë's intense interest in Thackeray, to whom she had dedicated the second edition of ' Jane Eyre ' is graphically described by Miss Thackeray :

She sat gazing at him with kindling eyes of interest, lighting up with a sort of illumination every now and then as she answered him. I can see her bending forward over the table not eating, but listening to what he said as he carved the dish before him.

Thackeray himself has drawn a touching picture of Charlotte Brontë as he first saw her :

'I saw her first,' he says, 'just as I rose out of an illness from which I had never thought to recover. I remember the trembling little frame, the little hand, the great honest eyes. An impetuous honesty seemed to me to characterise the woman.'

.   .   .   .

New to the London world, she entered it with an independent, indomitable spirit of her own ; and judged of contemporaries, and especially spied out arrogance and affectation, with extraordinary keenness of vision. She was angry with her favourites if their conduct or conversation fell below her ideal.

How Charlotte Brontë could ' chill ' a party is humorously described by Mrs Richmond Ritchie in her account of an evening reception given by her father in Charlotte Brontë's honour :

Every one waited for the brilliant conversation which never began at all. . . The room looked very dark, the lamp began to smoke a little, the conversation grew dimmer and more dim, the ladies sat round still expectant, my father was too much perturbed by the gloom and the silence to be able to cope with it at all.

At a later stage in the evening Miss Thackeray tells us how

I was surprised to see my father opening the front door with his hat on. He put his fingers to his lips, walked out into the darkness, and shut the door quietly behind him. When I went back to the drawing-room again the ladies asked me where he was. I vaguely answered that I thought he was coming back.

But he was not! He had given up his own party in

despair, and betaken himself to the consolations of a cigar at his club ! The gloom, the constraint, the general situation had overwhelmed him.

'The ladies,' says Miss Thackeray, 'waited, wondered, and finally departed also. As we were going up to bed with our candles after everybody was gone I remember two pretty Miss L——'s in shiny silk dresses arriving, full of expectation. We still said we thought our father would soon be back; but the Miss L——'s declined to wait upon the chance, laughed, and drove away.'

Mrs. Procter was accustomed to tell the story of that evening with much humour. It was, she always declared, 'one of the dullest evenings she ever spent in her life,' though she extracted much entertainment from it years afterwards. The failure of this attempt by Thackeray to entertain Charlotte Brontë illustrates one aspect of the character of both of them : in Charlotte Brontë her want of social gifts; in Thackeray his impatience of social discomfort.

Mrs. Brookfield, who was perfectly at home in any society, said that Charlotte Brontë was the the most difficult woman to talk to she had ever met. That evening at Thackeray's house she tried hard to enter into conversation with her. Mrs. Brookfield used to relate with some humour what she called 'my conversation with Charlotte Brontë.' She said, 'I opened it by saying I hoped she liked London ; to which Charlotte Brontë replied curtly, "I do and I don't." ' Naturally Mrs. Brookfield's audience used to wait for more, but, said Mrs. Brookfield, 'that is all.'

If Miss Brontë did not talk much, as was usual with her, she kept her eyes open. One of Mr. Thackeray's guests was Miss Adelaide Procter, and those who remember that lady's charming personality will not be surprised to learn that I was greatly attracted by her. During our drive home I was seated opposite to Miss Brontë, and I was startled by her leaning forward, putting her hands on my knees, and saying ' She would make you a very nice wife.' ' Whom do you mean?' I replied. ' Oh! you know whom I mean,' she said; and we relapsed into silence. Though I admired Miss Procter very much, it was not a case of love at first sight, as Miss Brontë supposed.

When I first asked Thackeray to dine to meet Charlotte Brontë, he offended her by failing to respect the anonymity behind which, at that time, she was very anxious to screen herself. On another occasion Thackeray roused the hidden fire in Charlotte Brontë's soul, and was badly scorched himself as the result. My mother and I had taken her to one of Thackeray's lectures on ' The English Humourists.' After the lecture Thackeray came down from the platform and shook hands with many of the audience, receiving their congratulations and compliments. He was in high spirits, and rather thoughtlessly said to his mother—Mrs. Carmichael Smyth—' Mother, you must allow me to introduce you to Jane Eyre.' This was uttered in a loud voice, audible over half the room. Everybody near turned round and stared at the disconcerted little lady, who grew confused and angry when she realised that every eye was fixed upon her. My mother got her away as quickly as possible.

On the next afternoon Thackeray called. I arrived at home shortly afterwards, and when I entered the drawing-room found a scene in full progress. Only these two were in the room. Thackeray was standing on the hearthrug, looking anything but happy. Charlotte Brontë stood close to him, with head thrown back and face white with anger. The first words I heard were, ' No, Sir! If *you* had come to our part of the country in Yorkshire, what would you have thought of me if I had introduced you to my father, before a mixed company of strangers, as " Mr. Warrington "? ' Thackeray replied, ' No, you

H 2

mean "Arthur Pendennis."' 'No, I *don't* mean Arthur Pendennis!' retorted Miss Brontë; 'I mean Mr. Warrington, and Mr. Warrington would not have behaved as you behaved to me yesterday.' The spectacle of this little woman, hardly reaching to Thackeray's elbow, but, somehow, looking stronger and fiercer than himself, and casting her incisive words at his head, resembled the dropping of shells into a fortress.

By this time I had recovered my presence of mind, and hastened to interpose. Thackeray made the necessary and half-humorous apologies, and the parting was a friendly one.

Thackeray shocked Charlotte Brontë sadly by the fashion of his talk on literary subjects. The truth is, Charlotte Brontë's heroics roused Thackeray's antagonism. He declined to pose on a pedestal for her admiration, and with characteristic contrariety of nature he seemed to be tempted to say the very things that set Charlotte Brontë's teeth, so to speak, on edge, and affronted all her ideals. He insisted on discussing his books very much as a clerk in a bank would discuss the ledgers he had to keep for a salary. But all this was, on Thackeray's part, an affectation: an affectation into which he was provoked by what he considered Charlotte Brontë's high falutin'. Miss Brontë wanted to persuade him that he was a great man with a 'misson;' and Thackeray, with many wicked jests, declined to recognise the ' mission.'

But, despite all this, Charlotte Brontë, much as she scolded Thackeray, never doubted his greatness. He was, she once said, ' a Titan in mind.'

Before Thackeray went to America in the autumn of 1852 I had a portrait of him made by Mr. Samuel Laurence as a present to his daughters. My mother took Charlotte Brontë to see it at the artist's studio. It was a very fine and expressive rendering of Thackeray's powerful head. Charlotte Brontë stood looking long upon

it in silence; and then, as if quoting the words un-
consciously, she said: 'There came up a lion out of
Judah.'

After Charlotte Brontë's first visit to our house her
anonymity was dropped, and people naturally tried to draw
her out. She shrank from this, or resented it, and seemed
to place herself under my mother's care for protection.
My mother accepted the position, and was generally equal
to it, but sometimes, when accident left Charlotte Brontë
exposed to a direct attack, the fire concealed beneath her
mildness broke out. The first time this happened I was
not a little surprised. G. H. Lewes, who was lunching
with us, had the indiscretion to say across the table,
'There ought to be a bond of sympathy between us, Miss
Brontë; for we have both written naughty books!' This
fired the train with a vengeance, and an explosion
followed. I listened with mingled admiration and alarm
to the indignant eloquence with which that impertinent
remark was answered.

By way of parenthesis, I may say that 'Jane Eyre'
was really considered in those days by many people to be
an immoral book. My mother told me one evening that
Lady Herschel, having found the book in her drawing-
room, said: 'Do you leave such a book as *this* about, at
the risk of your daughters reading it?' Charlotte Brontë
herself was quite unconscious that the book possessed, in
any degree, a reputation of this sort; and she was as much
surprised as affronted when Lady Eastlake—then Miss
Rigby—in her review of 'Jane Eyre' in the 'Quarterly
Review' (December 1848) brutally said that 'if it were
written by a woman, it must be by one who had forfeited
the right to the society of her sex.'

Charlotte Brontë had much nobility of character; she
had an almost exaggerated sense of duty; she was
scrupulously honest and perfectly just. When Sir James
Stephen, the father of the late Mr. Justice Stephen, said

to me during a long conversation I had with him at
Cambridge on a very delicate subject, 'I have lived a long
and not unobservant life, and I have never yet met with a
perfectly just woman,' I could not help thinking that he
had never met Charlotte Brontë. Miss Brontë was
critical of character, but not of action; this she judged
favourably and kindly. Generally, I thought, she put too
kind an interpretation on the actions of a friend.

As I have mentioned, my mother and sisters complained that Charlotte Brontë always seemed to them to
be noting and analysing· everything that was said and
everything that happened. That they were more or less
right can hardly be doubted, and the following extract
from a letter, written after her first visit to London to a
friend in New Zealand, and sent by her to Mrs. Gaskell—
who gave it to me—is a salient instance of Charlotte
Brontë's habit in this respect :

Mr. Smith's residence at Bayswater, six miles from Cornhill, is a very fine place. The rooms, the drawing-rooms
especially, looked splendid to us. There was no company, only
his mother, his two grown-up sisters, and his brother, a lad of
twelve or thirteen, and a little sister, the youngest of the family,
very like himself. They are all dark-eyed, dark-haired, and
have clear pale faces. The mother is a portly handsome
woman of her age, and all the children were more or less well-
looking, one of the daughters decidedly pretty. We had a fine
dinner, which neither Anne nor I had appetite to eat, and
were glad when it was over. I always feel under an awkward
constraint at table; dining out would be hideous to me. Mr.
Smith made himself very pleasant. He is a firm, intelligent
man of business, though so young; bent on getting on, and I
think desirous to make his way by fair honourable means. He
is enterprising, but likewise cool and cautious. Mr. Smith is a
practical man : I wish Mr. Williams were more so, but he is
altogether of the contemplative theorising order. Mr. Williams
has too many abstractions.

The 'fine place' in Bayswater was a house in Westbourne Place, now a street of shops. The house in which we lived is occupied by a hairdresser, and you may purchase cosmetics and hairpins in what used to be the dining-room, and have your hair cut, curled, singed, and shampooed in the little room in which I read the manuscript of 'Jane Eyre.'

'Villette' is full of scenes which one can trace to incidents which occurred during Miss Brontë's visits to us.

The scene at the theatre at Brussels in that book, and the description of the actress, were suggested by Rachel, whom we took her to see more than once. The scene of the fire comes from a slight accident to the scenery at Devonshire House, where Charles Dickens, Mr. Forster, and other men of letters gave a performance. I took Charlotte Brontë and one of my sisters to Devonshire House, and when the performance, which was for a charity, was repeated, I took another of my sisters, who had been too unwell to go on the first occasion, and a Miss D. At one stage of the second performance the scenery caught fire. There was some risk of a general panic, and I took my sister and Miss D. each by the wrist, and held them down till the panic had ceased. I seem to have written a description of the occurrence to Miss Brontë, for I find that she refers to it in one of her letters, saying, ' It is easy to realise the scene.'

In 'Villette' my mother was the original of 'Mrs. Bretton ; ' several of her expressions are given *verbatim*. I myself, as I discovered, stood for 'Dr. John.' Charlotte Brontë admitted this to Mrs. Gaskell, to whom she wrote : ' I was kept waiting longer than usual for Mr. Smith's opinion of the book, and I was rather uneasy, for I was afraid he had found me out, and was offended.'

During Miss Brontë's visit to us in June 1850, I persuaded her to sit to Mr. George Richmond for her portrait. This I sent afterwards with an engraving of the portrait of the Duke of Wellington to her father, who was much pleased with them.

Mr. Richmond mentioned that when she saw the portrait (she was not allowed to see it before it was finished) she burst into tears, exclaiming that it was so like her sister Anne, who had died the year before.

At the conclusion of this visit I had to take a young brother to Scotland. I was accompanied by my sister, and with some difficulty I induced Miss Brontë to meet us in Edinburgh. I think the visit was very agreeable and interesting to her. We were fortunate in getting a driver, whom we engaged for the whole of our visit, who knew every interesting nook and corner in Edinburgh, who was better read in Scottish history and the Waverley Novels than I was, and whose dry humour exactly suited Miss Brontë. We left her in Yorkshire on our way back to London.

Towards the end of 1853 I was engaged to be married, and wrote to inform Miss Brontë of the fact. Her reply was brief, but she afterwards wrote more at length on the subject, when informing me of her engagement to Mr. Nicholls.

I thank you for your congratulations and good wishes ; if these last are realised but in part I shall be very thankful. It gave me also sincere pleasure to be assured of your happiness, though of that I never doubted. I have faith also in its permanent character—provided Mrs. George Smith is—what it pleases me to fancy her to be. You never told me any particulars about her, though I should have liked them much, but did not like to ask questions, knowing how much your mind and time would be engaged. What *I* have to say is soon told.

The step in contemplation is no hasty one; on the gentleman's side at least, it has been meditated for many years, and I hope that, in at last acceding to it, I am acting right; it is what I earnestly wish to do. My future husband is a clergyman. He was for eight years my father's curate. He left because the idea of this marriage was not entertained as he wished. His departure was regarded by the parish as a calamity, for he had devoted himself to his duties with no ordinary diligence. Various circumstances have led my father to consent to his return, nor can I deny that my own feelings have been much impressed and changed by the nature and strength of the qualities brought out in the course of his long attachment. I fear I must accuse myself of having formerly done him less than justice. However, he is to come back now. He has foregone many chances of preferment to return to the obscure village of Haworth. I believe I do right in marrying him. I mean to try to make him a good wife. There has been heavy anxiety—but I begin to hope all will end for the best. My expectations, however, are very subdued—very different, I dare say, to what *yours* were before you were married. Care and Fear stand so close to Hope, I sometimes scarcely even see her for the shadows they cast. And yet I am thankful too, and the doubtful Future must be left with Providence.

On one feature in the marriage I can dwell with *unmingled* satisfaction, with a *certainty* of being right. It takes nothing from the attention I owe to my father. I am not to leave him ; my future husband consents to come here—thus papa secures by the step a devoted and reliable assistant in his old age.

There can, of course, be no reason for withholding the intelligence from your mother and sisters ; remember me kindl to them whenever you write.

I hardly know in what form of greeting to include your wife's name, as I have never seen her. Say to her whatever may seem to you most appropriate and most expressive of good-will.

Yours sincerely,
C. BRONTË.

Miss Brontë and my wife never met. She was married to the Rev. Arthur B. Nicholls on June 29, 1854, and died on March 31, 1855.

OUR BIRTH AND PARENTAGE

Reprinted from the 'Cornhill Magazine,' January 1901

IF periodicals may be said to have birthdays, this is a 'Cornhill Magazine' birthday. As has been recorded by the graceful pen of Mrs. Richmond Ritchie, the first number was published in January 1860. Mrs. Richmond Ritchie writes of her impressions of the event from the home of the editor, and gives a charming picture of the domestic excitement caused by her father's new experience in editorship. My recollections are generally of a more matter-of-fact character, and must needs be related in a more commonplace manner.

Early in 1859 I conceived the idea of founding a new magazine. The plan flashed upon me suddenly, as did most of the ideas which have in the course of my life led to successful operations. The existing magazines were few, and when not high-priced were narrow in literary range, and it seemed to me that a shilling magazine which contained, in addition to other first-class literary matter, a serial novel by Thackeray must command a large sale. Thackeray's name was one to conjure with, and according to the plan, as it shaped itself in my mind, the public would have a serial novel by Thackeray, and a good deal else well worth reading, for the price they had been accustomed to pay for the monthly numbers of his novels alone.

I had, at first, no idea of securing Thackeray as editor. In spite of all his literary gifts I did not attribute to him the business qualities which go to make a good editor. But a novel by Thackeray was essential to my scheme. I wrote on a slip of paper the terms I was prepared to offer for his co-operation, and I went to him with it. I had previously published ' Esmond,' ' The Kickleburys on the Rhine,' 'The English Humourists of the Eighteenth Century,' ' The Rose and the Ring,' and I had an impression that Thackeray liked my mode of transacting business. I said I wanted him to read a little memorandum, and added, ' I wonder whether you will consider it, or will at once consign it to your wastepaper-basket ! '

Here are the *ipsissima verba* of my proposal :

' Smith, Elder, & Co. have it in contemplation to commence the publication of a Monthly Magazine on January 1st, 1860. They are desirous of inducing Mr. Thackeray to contribute to their periodical, and they make the following proposal to Mr. Thackeray :

' 1. That he shall write either one or two novels of the ordinary size for publication in the Magazine—one-twelfth portion of each novel (estimated to be about equal to one number of a serial) to appear in each number of the Magazine.

' 2. That Mr. Thackeray shall assign to Smith, Elder, & Co. the right to publish the novels in their Magazine and in a separate form afterwards, and to all sums to be received for the work from American and Continental Publishers.

' 3. That Smith, Elder, & Co. shall pay Mr. Thackeray 350*l*. each month.

' 4. That the profits of all editions of the novels published at a lower price than the first edition shall be equally divided between Mr. Thackeray and Smith, Elder, & Co.

' 65 CORNHILL : *February 19th*, 1859.'

Thackeray read the slip carefully, and, with character-istic absence of guile, allowed me to see that he regarded the terms as phenomenal. When he had finished reading the paper, he said with a droll smile : ' I am not going to put such a document as *this* into my wastepaper-basket.'

We had a little talk of an explanatory kind, and he agreed to consider my proposal. He subsequently accepted it, and the success of this part of my plans was assured.

My next step was to secure an editor. I applied in the first instance to Mr. Tom Hughes, who received me with the genial manner for which he was remarkable, but he would not say 'Yes.' He had thrown in his lot, he explained, with Macmillan's, and with characteristic loyalty did not feel free to take other literary work. Several other names came under consideration, but none seemed to be exactly suitable, and I was at my wits' end. All my plans, indeed, were 'hung up,' pending the engagement of an editor. We were then living at Wimbledon, and I used to ride on the Common before breakfast. One morning, just as I had pulled up my horse after a smart gallop, that good genius which has so often helped me whispered into my ear, 'Why should not Mr. Thackeray edit the magazine, you yourself doing what is necessary to supplement any want of business qualifications on his part? You know that he has a fine literary judgment, a great reputation with men of letters as well as with the public, and any writer would be proud to contribute to a periodical under his editorship.'

After breakfast I drove straight to Thackeray's house in Onslow Square, talked to him of my difficulty, and induced him to accept the editorship, for which he was to receive a salary of 1,000l. a year.

Then I set to work with energy to make the undertaking a success. We secured the most brilliant contributors from every quarter. Our terms were lavish almost to the point of recklessness. No pains and no cost were spared to make the new magazine the best periodical yet known to English literature.

The name of the ' Cornhill Magazine ' was suggested by Thackeray, and was, at the time, much ridiculed. Sarcastic journalists asked whether it suited the ' dignity '

of literature to label a magazine with the name of a street ?
Should we not next have such periodicals as 'The Smith-
field Review,' or 'The Leadenhall Market Magazine'?
But the name 'Cornhill Magazine' really set the example
of quite a new class of titles for periodicals—titles that
linked the magazines that bore them to historic localities
in London, where perhaps they were published.   Thus we
have since had 'Temple Bar,' 'Belgravia,' 'St. Pauls
Magazine,' the 'Strand,' &c., &c.

Thackeray wrote an excellent advertisement of the
new magazine, in the form of a letter which is worth
reproducing.

'The Cornhill Magazine,' Smith, Elder, & Co.
65, *Cornhill, November* 1, 1859.

A LETTER FROM THE EDITOR TO A FRIEND AND CONTRIBUTOR.

DEAR ——.   Our Store-House being in Cornhill, we date
and name our Magazine from its place of publication.   We
might have assumed a title much more startling : for example,
'The Thames on Fire' was a name suggested ; and, placarded
in red letters about the City, and Country, it would no doubt
have excited some curiosity.   But, on going to London Bridge,
the expectant rustic would have found the stream rolling on
its accustomed course, and would have turned away angry at
being hoaxed.   Sensible people are not to be misled by fine
prospectuses and sounding names ; the present Writer has
been for five-and-twenty years before the world, which has
taken his measure pretty accurately.   We are too long
acquainted to try and deceive one another ; and were I to
propose any such astounding feat as that above announced, I
know quite well how the schemer would be received, and the
scheme would end.

You, then, who ask what 'The Cornhill Magazine' is to be,
and what sort of articles you shall supply for it ?—if you were
told that the Editor, known hitherto only by his published
writings, was in reality a great reformer, philosopher, and wise-
acre, about to expound prodigious doctrines and truths until
now unrevealed, to guide and direct the peoples, to pull down
the existing order of things, to edify new social or political

structures, and, in a word, to set the Thames on Fire; if you heard such designs ascribed to him—*risum teneatis ?* You know I have no such pretensions : but, as an Author who has written long, and had the good fortune to find a very great number of readers, I think I am not mistaken in supposing that they give me credit for experience and observation, for having lived with educated people in many countries, and seen the world in no small variety; and, having heard me soliloquise, with so much kindness and favour, and say my own say about life, and men and women, they will not be unwilling to try me as Conductor of a Concert, in which I trust many skilful performers will take part.

We hope for a large number of readers, and must seek, in the first place, to amuse and interest them. Fortunately for some folks, novels are as daily bread to others ; and fiction of course must form a part, but only a part, of our entertainment. We want, on the other hand, as much reality as possible— discussion and narrative of events interesting to the public, personal adventures and observations, familiar reports of scientific discovery, description of Social Institutions—*quicquid agunt homines*—a ' Great Eastern,' a battle in China, a Race-Course, a popular Preacher—there is hardly any subject we *don't* want to hear about, from lettered and instructed men who are competent to speak on it.

I read the other day in ' The Illustrated London News ' (in my own room at home), that I was at that moment at Bordeaux, purchasing first-class claret for first-class contributors, and second class for those of inferior *cru.* Let me adopt this hospitable simile ; and say that at our contributors' table, I do not ask or desire to shine especially myself, but to take my part occasionally, and to invite pleasant and instructed gentlemen and ladies to contribute their share to the conversation.   It may be a Foxhunter who has the turn to speak ; or a Geologist, Engineer, Manufacturer, Member of the House of Commons, Lawyer, Chemist—what you please.   If we can only get people to tell what they know, pretty briefly and good-humouredly, and not in a manner obtrusively didactic, what a pleasant ordinary we may have, and how gladly folks will come to it !   If our friends have good manners, a good education, and write in good English, the company, I am sure, will be all the better pleased ; and the guests, whatever their rank, age, sex be, will be glad to be addressed by well-educated gentlemen and women. A professor ever so learned, a curate in his country retirement, an artisan after work-hours, a schoolmaster or mistress when the children are gone home, or the young ones themselves when their lessons are over, may like to hear what the world is talking about, or be brought into friendly communication with persons whom the world knows. There are points on which agreement is impossible, and on these we need not touch. At our social table, we shall suppose the ladies and children always present; we shall not set rival politicians by the ears; we shall listen to every guest who has an apt word to say; and, I hope, induce clergymen of various denominations to say grace in their turn. The kindly fruits of the earth, which grow for all—may we not enjoy them with friendly hearts? The field is immensely wide; the harvest perennial, and rising everywhere; we can promise competent fellow-labourers a welcome and a good wage; and hope a fair custom from the public for our stores at 'THE CORNHILL MAGAZINE.'

W. M. THACKERAY.

The cover of the magazine, designed by Mr. Godfrey Sykes, a young student at the South Kensington Schools of Art, had the good fortune to strike the popular taste, and I still think it most effective. When I showed the sketch of the cover to Thackeray, he said: 'What a lovely design! I hope you have given the man a good cheque!' The only complaint that has ever been made against the design is that the sower shown in it is sowing with his left hand. But a sower uses his hands alternately. He goes down the row scattering with his right hand, and as he comes back he scatters with his left. I was in the country just after this criticism on the design appeared in the papers, and actually saw a man sowing with his left hand; and, of course, I made the most of the circumstance.

It was arranged that Thackeray was to write 'Lovel the Widower' for the magazine; but we thought it well to secure a second novel, and decided on asking Anthony Trollope to write a serial.

In his 'Autobiography' Trollope describes his astonishment at finding the 'Cornhill Magazine,' after its advent had been announced so long, still unsupplied with a serial, and he quotes this as a proof of Thackeray's incorrigible habit of loitering. 'Framley Parsonage,' he says, had to take the foremost place in the new magazine in default of a novel which Thackeray *ought* to have written but did not. But there was no default on Thackeray's part. His 'Lovel the Widower,' as had been arrangea, made its appearance in the first number of the 'Cornhill.' 'Framley Parsonage' was given the place of honour in the new magazine by Thackeray's own arrangement and on the grounds of pure courtesy; it was exactly as a host would invite a guest to walk into a room before himself. This is an example of Thackeray's quaint and chivalrous courtesy in literary matters. He would not claim the first place in his own magazine. He looked upon himself as the host, and upon Trollope as his guest.

It occurred to me that if I could secure Tennyson as a regular contributor to the new magazine he would prove a great attraction. His 'Idylls of the King' had not long appeared, and I thought I would ask him to write for us another set of 'Idylls.' Tennyson was then on a visit to Mrs. Cameron on Putney Heath, and I wrote to ask if I might call upon him on a matter of business. He made an appointment, and during our interview, I offered to pay him five thousand guineas for as many lines as were contained in the 'Idylls of the King' (in fact for 4,750 lines), on condition that the poems should be printed in the 'Cornhill Magazine' and that I should publish them for three years afterwards. That offer was really a 'record' as far as the market rates of poetry up to that time were concerned. When compared with anything Tennyson had yet received for his poems it might fairly be described as extravagant.

Tennyson listened to my proposal with entire calmness.

He asked me to smoke with him and chatted pleasantly; but gave me no idea as to whether my offer was acceptable. Mrs. Tennyson presently came into the room, and Tennyson addressing her, said: ' My dear, we are much richer than we thought we were. Mr. Smith has just offered me five thousand guineas for a book the size of the "Idylls." And,' he continued, 'if Mr. Smith offers five thousand, of course the book is worth ten!' A remark at which we all laughed. Nothing came of this proposal, which I had no temptation to renew after the rapid success achieved by the magazine. But Thackeray obtained from Tennyson his fine poem ' Tithonus ' for the second number.

We had secured a quite remarkable body of contributors: public attention was keenly fixed on the new venture, and when the first number appeared in January 1860 the sale was astonishing. It was the literary event of the year. Along Cornhill nothing was to be seen but people carrying bundles of the orange-coloured magazine. Of the first number some 120,000 copies were sold, a number then without precedent in English serial literature.

The exhilarating effect of this success on its editor is amusingly described by Mr. James T. Fields in his ' Yesterdays with Authors.' Mr. Fields says:

'The enormous circulation achieved by the "Cornhill Magazine," when it was first started with Thackeray for its editor-in-chief, is a matter of literary history. The announcement by his publishers that a sale of a hundred and ten thousand of the first number had been reached made the editor half delirious with joy, and he ran away to Paris to be rid of the excitement for a few days. I met him by appointment at his hotel in the Rue de la Paix, and found him wild with exultation and full of enthusiasm for excellent George Smith, his publisher. " London," he exclaimed, " is not big enough to contain me now, and I am obliged to add Paris to my residence! Great heavens," said he, throwing up his long arms, " where will this

I

tremendous circulation stop! Who knows but that I shall
have to add Vienna and Rome to my whereabouts? If the
worst comes to the worst, New York, also, may fall into my
clutches, and only the Rocky Mountains may be able to stop
my progress!" Those days in Paris with him were simply
tremendous. We dined at all possible and impossible places
together. We walked round and round the glittering court of
the Palais Royal, gazing in at the windows of the jewellers'
shops, and all my efforts were necessary to restrain him from
rushing in and ordering a pocketful of diamonds and "other
trifles," as he called them; "for," said he, "how can I spend
the princely income which Smith allows me for editing the
'Cornhill,' unless I begin instantly somewhere?" If he saw a
group of three or four persons talking together in an excited
way, after the manner of that then *riant* Parisian people, he
would whisper to me with immense gesticulation: "There,
there, you see the news has reached Paris, and perhaps the
number has gone up since my last accounts from London."
His spirits during those few days were colossal, and he told me
that he found it impossible to sleep, "for counting up his
subscribers."'

The success of the 'Cornhill' was so far beyond
my expectation that I thought that its editor ought to
share in the fruits of that success; I told Mr. Thackeray
he must allow me to double his editorial payment. He
seemed much touched by my communication. I have
said that our payments to contributors were lavish. As
figures are generally interesting, I may mention that the
largest amount expended on the literature of a single
number was 1,183l. 3s. 8d. (August 1862), and the total
expenditure under that head for the first four years
was 32,280l. 11s., the illustrations costing in addition
4,376l. 11s.

The largest payment made for a novel was 7,000l., to
Mrs. Lewes (George Eliot) for 'Romola.' The largest
payment made for short articles was 12l. 12s. a page to
Mr. Thackeray, for his 'Roundabout Papers.' In regard
to the payment to Mrs. Lewes, an incident seems to

deserve honourable record as a signal proof of the author's artistic sensibility. Mrs. Lewes read part of ' Romola ' to me, and anyone who has heard that lady read and remembers her musical and sympathetic voice will understand that the MS. lost nothing in effect by her reading. On the following day I offered her 10,000*l.* for the book for the 'Cornhill Magazine,' and for a limited right to subsequent publication. It was stipulated that the book should form sixteen numbers of twenty-four pages each. Before the appearance of the first part Mrs. Lewes said that she found that she could not properly divide the book into as many as sixteen parts. I took exception to this alteration of our arrangement, and pointed out that my offer was based on the book being in sixteen parts, and that my calculations were made with regard to the magazine being able to afford a payment of so much a number. She said that she quite understood that the alteration would make a difference to me, but that she supposed the amount of the difference could easily be calculated. George Lewes and I did all we possibly could to persuade her to reconsider her decision, but in vain. We pointed out to her that the publication in the magazine was ephemeral, and that the work would be published in a separate form afterwards and be judged as a whole. However, nothing could move her, and she preferred receiving 7,000*l.* in place of 10,000*l.* for the book. ' Romola ' did not increase the sale of the magazine ; it is difficult to say what, if any, effect it had in sustaining the sale. As a separate publication it had not, I think, the success it deserved.

The first novel written by Miss Thackeray, the charming ' Story of Elizabeth,' appeared in the ' Cornhill Magazine' towards the end of 1862. As I was coming away from her father one morning early in that year, she slipped out of the dining-room, put a packet into my hand, said in a pretty, shy manner, ' Will you, please, read this, Mr. Smith?' and disappeared. The packet contained the 'Story of Elizabeth'; after reading it I had it put into type for the 'Cornhill,' and sent a proof to her father. When I next saw him I asked if he had read it. 'No,' he said; 'I tried to, but I broke down.' This was only one of a thousand indications of Thackeray's sensibility and of the great love between the father and daughter.

The first article Miss Thackeray wrote for the Magazine was called 'Little Scholars,' and was printed in the fifth number. Thackeray sent it to me with a letter containing the following passage :

'And in the meantime comes a little contribution called "Little Scholars," which I send you and which moistened my paternal spectacles. It is the article I talked of sending to "Blackwood"; but why should "Cornhill" lose such a sweet paper, because it was my dear girl who wrote it? Papas, however, are bad judges—you decide whether we shall have it or not!'

I find a characteristic postscript to this letter :

'Mrs. C—— growls—is satisfied—says she shan't write any more—and invites me to dinner.'

I must say that I think our success was well deserved. Our contributors gave the new magazine of their very best. No other group equally brilliant had ever been brought together before within the covers of one magazine. During the first year there were articles from the following writers :

ANTHONY TROLLOPE	MRS. ARCHER CLIVE
SIR JOHN BOWRING	M. J. HIGGINS ('JACOB
G. H. LEWES	OMNIUM')
REV. F. MAHONY ('FATHER	THOMAS HOOD
PROUT')	ALFRED TENNYSON
SIR JOHN BURGOYNE	GEORGE AUGUSTUS SALA
THORNTON HUNT	R. MONCKTON MILNES
ALLEN YOUNG	MRS. GASKELL

FREDERICK GREENWOOD	GEORGE MACDONALD
HERMAN MERIVALE	JAMES HINTON
REV. S. R. HOLE	MATTHEW ARNOLD
JOHN RUSKIN	MRS. BROWNING
ADELAIDE PROCTER	SIR JOHN W. KAYE
HENRY COLE	FITZJAMES STEPHEN
E. S. DALLAS	EDWARD TOWNSEND
ALBERT SMITH	T. ADOLPHUS TROLLOPE
JOHN HOLLINGSHEAD	LORD LYTTON
SIR HENRY THOMPSON	CHARLES LEVER
LAURENCE OLIPHANT	FREDERICK LOCKER
MISS THACKERAY	

The 'Cornhill Magazine' during many years contained illustrations, and it was no less distinguished for its artistic merit than for its literature. Among the artists whose drawings appeared in the magazine were the following:

JOHN EVERETT MILLAIS	F. W. BURTON
F. SANDYS	S. L. FILDES
F. LEIGHTON	HUBERT HERKOMER
RICHARD DOYLE	G. D. LESLIE
FREDERICK WALKER	MARCUS STONE
GEORGE DU MAURIER	MRS. ALLINGHAM
SIR NOEL PATON	F. DICKSEE
CHARLES KEENE	E. J. PINWELL

I may possibly at a future time ask the Editor of the 'Cornhill Magazine' to allow me to submit to him a few jottings from my memory of some of these writers and artists.

Although we did our best to make the new venture a success, yet accidents will happen, and the launch of the 'Cornhill' was attended with one somewhat exasperating business blunder. When I had got the first number ready for press I was rather knocked up, and went with my wife for a three weeks' holiday to the Lakes. Those three weeks indirectly cost us a considerable loss in the advertising pages of the 'Cornhill.' I left instructions with my staff not to make any advertising contracts without reference to me. They received offers extending over twelve months at 6*l.* 6*s.* or 7*l.* 7*s.* a page—sufficiently good rates for magazines with the ordinary circulation. They forwarded these proposals to me, intimating that unless they heard from me to the contrary by a given date they would close with them. There was delay in the letter reaching me, and the contracts were made at those rates. But with the circulation reached by the ' Cornhill ' the mere printing and paper cost us much more than the amounts we were to receive under the contracts. When I returned to London I made the rate twenty guineas per page.

In this connection I had a rather curious exposition of the science of advertising. The rate we charged was high ; but measured against our circulation it was really much lower than that of any other magazine ; and I was a little surprised that, considering the enormous publicity our pages offered to advertisers, they were not better filled. I found myself at a dinner-party sitting next to a well-known advertiser, and I thought I would try to get a solution of the puzzle. I began by saying I was not a canvasser for advertisements, but I wanted information. ' You advertise largely,' I said, ' in a certain magazine. You pay five guineas a page, and you know that the circulation of that magazine is not 10,000 copies. The "Cornhill" has a circulation of more than 100,000 copies; we charge twenty guineas a page for advertisements ; yet I don't find that advertisements come in to the extent I expected. If a circulation of 10,000 copies is worth five guineas a page, a circulation of 100,000 copies ought to be worth fifty guineas a page. And as we only charge twenty guineas, our rates are, proportionately, lower by more than fifty per cent. than those of other magazines. Why don't advertisers take advantage of what we offer ? ' ' Ah ! ' said the great advertiser, ' you evidently know nothing about it' ; and he proceeded to expound to me, on the authority of his large experience, the true secret of advertising.

'We don't consider,' he said, ' that an advertisement seen for the first time by a reader is worth anything. The second time it is seen counts for a little—not much. The third time the reader's attention is arrested; the fourth time he reads the advertisement through ; the fifth time he is probably a purchaser. It takes time to soak in. It is the number of the impressions that tells. Now you see,' he said, ' I can advertise five times in most magazines for twenty-five guineas ; but five times in the "Cornhill" would cost me 100 guineas.'

This theory that it takes a *number* of impressions to make an advertisement effective is, perhaps, correct. I certainly had had an example of what my interlocutor meant many years previously, during my drives twice a week to Box Hill, to see my father during his last illness. On a tree by the roadside was a flaming placard, announcing some trumpery penny publication. The placard depicted a young woman, with long black hair, thrusting a dagger into the heart of a ruffianly looking man, with the blood spurting all over the neighbourhood. When I first saw the placard my eyes scarcely dwelt for a moment on it. It awakened no curiosity. But after seeing it twice a week for six weeks, that girl's figure had so ' soaked in ' that I felt impelled to go and buy the publication.

We lightened our labours in the service of the ' Cornhill ' by monthly dinners. The principal contributors used to assemble at my table in Gloucester Square every month while we were in London ; and these ' Cornhill ' dinners were very delightful and interesting. Thackeray always attended, though he was often in an indifferent state of health. At one of these dinners Trollope was to meet Thackeray for the first time, and was eagerly looking

forward to an introduction to him. Just before dinner I
took him up to Thackeray and introduced him with
suitable *empressement*. Thackeray curtly said, 'How do?'
and, to my wonder and Trollope's anger, turned on his
heel! He was suffering at the time from an ailment
which, at that particular moment, caused him a sudden
spasm of pain; though we, of course, could not know this.
I well remember the expression on Trollope's face at that
moment, and no one who knew Trollope will doubt that
he *could* look furious on an adequate—and sometimes on
an inadequate—occasion! He came to me the next morning in a very wrathful mood, and said that, had it not been
that he was in my house for the first time, he would have
walked out of it. He vowed he would never speak to
Thackeray again, and so forth. I did my best to soothe
him; though rather violent and irritable, he had a fine
nature with a substratum of great kindliness, and I believe
he left my room in a happier frame of mind than when
he entered it. He and Thackeray afterwards became
close friends.

These 'Cornhill' dinners gave rise to another incident
which at this distance of time seems trivial enough, but
which, at the moment, caused some indignation in my
own immediate circle.

Mr. Edmund Yates, who had had a dispute with
Thackeray which ended in Mr. Yates's compulsory withdrawal from the Garrick Club, did me the honour of
writing an article for a New York paper disparaging the
'Cornhill Magazine,' making a false statement as to its
falling circulation, and describing one of these dinners,
at none of which he was present. Yates represented
me as a good man of business, but an entirely unread
person; and, by way of throwing ridicule on the 'Cornhill'
functions, told—or rather mistold—a story of what had
been said at one of the dinners.

The story in the New York paper was made the subject

of an article, of the sneering type, in the 'Saturday Review.' The 'Saturday Review's' article left me quite undisturbed, but my wife, who was ill at the time, was much annoyed, and Thackeray, with generous sympathy, rebuked the 'Saturday' in a brilliant 'Roundabout Paper' entitled 'On Screens in Dining Rooms.' 'That a publisher should be criticised for his dinners, and for the conversations that did *not* take place there, is this,' asked Thackeray, 'tolerable press practice, legitimate joking, or honourable warfare?' Shortly after the 'Saturday Review' article appeared, Trollope walked into my room and said he had come to confess that *he* had given Yates the information on which his article was founded. He expressed the deepest regret, and said: 'I told the story, not against you, but against Thackeray.' I am afraid I answered him rather angrily. Trollope, however, took it very meekly, and said: 'I know I have done wrong, and you may say anything you like to me.'

The house at which these 'Cornhill' dinners took place had been previously occupied by Mr. Sadleir, notorious for his frauds, who was found dead on Hampstead Heath with a silver cream-jug by his side which had contained prussic acid. By some defect in the construction of the house, when the front door was opened the drawing-room door also slowly opened, and the wind lifted the carpet in slight waves. Thackeray, whose humour was sometimes of a grim sort, was never tired of suggesting that it was Sadleir's ghost come in search of some deeds which had been hidden under the floor. Why, he would demand in anxious tones, did I not have the carpet taken up and the deeds discovered? He pretended to account for my indifference on the subject to his own satisfaction by saying: 'I suppose you think any deeds you find will be forged?'[1]

'Two years since I had the good fortune to partake of some admirable dinners in Tyburnia—magnificent dinners indeed, but rendered doubly inter-

The monthly dinners were not our only alleviations of the regular routine of business.   Whenever any new literary arrangement with Mr. Thackeray was pending, he would playfully suggest that he always found his mind clearer for business at Greenwich than elsewhere, especially if his digestion were assisted by a certain brown hock, at 15s. a bottle, which Mr. Hart, the landlord, used to produce.   On these occasions Sir Charles Taylor, a very agreeable and prominent member of the Garrick Club, a friend of Thackeray and an acquaintance of mine, was always present.   Beyond an occasional witticism, Sir Charles Taylor did not take part in our negotiations (and, indeed, there was no negotiation, for I cannot remember a single instance in which Mr. Thackeray demurred to any proposal that I made to him), but his social gifts made our little dinners very pleasant.   One little anecdote may indicate the somewhat unconventional manner in which the business of the ' Cornhill Magazine ' was occasionally treated. Trollope came to me in Pall Mall, where we had now a branch office, to arrange for a new serial.   I told him my terms, but he demurred to my offer of 2,000l., and said that he had hoped for 3,000l.   I shook my head.   ' Well,' he replied, ' let us toss for that other 1,000l.'   I asked him if

esting from the fact that the house was that occupied by the late Mr. Sadleir. One night the late Mr. Sadleir took tea in that dining-room, and, to the surprise of his butler, went out, having put into his pocket his own cream-jug.   The next morning, you know, he was found dead on Hampstead Heath, with the cream-jug lying by him, into which he had poured the poison by which he died.   The idea of the ghost of the late gentleman flitting about the room gave a strange interest to the banquet.   Can you fancy him taking his tea alone in the dining-room?   He empties that cream-jug and puts it in his pocket ; and then he opens yonder door, through which he is never to pass again.   Now he crosses the hall : and hark ! the hall door shuts upon him, and his steps die away.   They are gone into the night.   They traverse the sleeping city.   They lead him into the fields, where the grey morning is beginning to glimmer.   He pours something from a bottle into a little silver jug.   It touches his lips, the lying lips.   Do they quiver a prayer ere that awful draught is swallowed ?   When the sun rises they are dumb. —*Roundabout Papers.*

he wished to ruin me, and said that if my banker heard of my tossing authors for their copyrights he would certainly close my account; and what about my clerks? How I should demoralise them if they suspected me of tossing with an author for his manuscript! We ultimately came to an agreement on my terms, which were sufficiently liberal. But I felt uncomfortable—I felt mean—I had refused a challenge. To relieve my mind I said, 'Now that is settled, if you will come over the way to my club, where we can have a little room to ourselves for five minutes, I will toss you for 1,000*l*. with pleasure.' Mr. Trollope did not accept the offer.

The large numbers of copies printed obliged us to go to press earlier in the month than most of the magazines, and we found some difficulty in getting articles up to time. There was an article by Mr. George Augustus Sala which was very much behind time, and the printer came to me with a long face. I said that I would call on Mr. Sala on my way to the City and try to get the article. I did call, and I knocked at the door of his chambers first with my knuckles and then with the knob of my stick, but without effect. There was no response. As I was going downstairs I met a friend of Sala whom I knew. 'If you are going to see Sala,' I said, 'you need not go upstairs, he's not there.' 'Do you want to see him?' he asked. 'Indeed I do,' said I. 'Then come up with me.' There was no knocking at the door this time; my friend produced a penny and put it into the slot which had been made for a letter-box. It had hardly ceased rolling on the floor before Sala appeared. He had only a page or two of his article to write, and I waited for it and carried it off. I had no idea of Mr. Sala's reason for 'sporting his oak' in this peculiar manner, and he did not vouchsafe any explanation.

The 'Cornhill' was edited by Thackeray from January 1860 to May 1862. I cannot truly say that he was, in a business sense, a good editor, and I had to do some part of the work myself. This was a pleasure to me, for I had the greatest possible admiration and affection for him. Such a relation between editor and publisher would have worked ill in the case of some men ; but Thackeray's nature was so generous, and my regard for him was so sincere, that no misunderstanding between us ever arose.

I used to drive round to his house in Onslow Square nearly every morning, and we discussed manuscripts and subjects together. Later in the day frequently came little notes, of which I have a large number, and of which the following is a characteristic specimen :

'36 O. S., S.W. : Jan. 1, 1861.

'My dear S.,—

' H. N. Y. to all Smiths.

' I am afraid we can't get Loch. He has been advised not to write except his own book, whatever that may be.

' Stephen can't do anything for Feb.

' Wynter says he will do Bread.

' This is all the present news from

'Yours ever,

'W. M. T.'

Thackeray was far too tender-hearted to be happy as an editor. He could not say ' No ' without himself suffering a pang as keen as that inflicted by his ' No ' on the rejected contributor. He would take pains—such as, I believe, few editors have ever taken—to soften his refusal. The beautiful letter to Mrs. Browning, printed in Mrs. Ritchie's article before mentioned, is an example of the pains that he took in writing to the contributors of rejected articles.

Thackeray poured out his sorrows as an editor in one of his ' Roundabout Papers.' It is entitled ' Thorns in the Cushion,' and is a good example of Thackeray's humour and an illustration of the effect upon him of editorial duties. No one can read the article without realising as I did that Mr. Thackeray came to a wise decision when he resigned the editorship of the magazine and thus consulted his own comfort and peace of mind.

I like to think that the tender heart of this noble man of genius was not troubled by editorial thorns during the remainder of his life. But in looking back it sometimes comes to me with a feeling akin to remorse that I was the instrument of imposing on him an uncongenial task, and that I might have done more than I did to relieve him of its burden.

IV

LAWFUL PLEASURES

Reprinted from the 'Cornhill Magazine,' February 1901

To most men few things are more disagreeable than litigation, and from litigation of the ordinary kind I am as averse as other people. Indeed, I am able to understand and sympathise with a well-known broker of Mincing Lane who, whenever threatened with litigation, is said to produce his cheque-book and ask how much there is to pay. There is only one form of litigation in which I have been engaged, and that is in the defence of actions for libel, and I must confess to looking back on my experience of the courts of law as having been interesting and even enjoyable. There is a certain pleasurable excitement in being defendant in such actions, it being granted that the libeller conscientiously believes that the libel is true in substance and in fact, and that he has done a public service by its publication.

There are other kinds of libel; for instance, the innocent libel—where there has been no intention on the part of the writer of libelling any one ; and the accidental libel, arising from a slip of the pen. An example of the first kind of libel is to be found in 'Plantagenet Harrison *v.* Smith, Elder, & Co.,' and of the second in the peril in which I stood by the accidental insertion in the ' Pall Mall Gazette ' of the name of the Credit Foncier for that of another company. The first afforded me no pleasure : on the contrary, I wrote a cheque for the damages and costs with 'most igstreme disgust'; and the second gave me a bad quarter of an hour.

When I was proprietor of the 'Pall Mall Gazette' I had to defend in Court three actions for libel, and my publisher had once to appear before the magistrate at Great Marlborough Street Police Court: as proprietor of the 'Cornhill Magazine' I have had to defend one action. As to the number of actions with which I have been threatened, some of them being carried nearly to the doors of the law courts, my memory does not serve me. But I remember that I invariably suffered genuine disappointment when I was informed by my solicitor that a plaintiff had withdrawn from proceedings.

The first and most important libel action which I was called upon to defend was that of Hunter v. Sharpe (Sharpe being the publisher of the 'Pall Mall Gazette') in the autumn of 1866. It is still interesting as an illustration of the functions and perils of a newspaper. There was a certain Dr. Hunter, who appended M.D. to his name—though he only had an American degree—and who advertised to an enormous extent in the newspapers a 'cure for consumption.' The advertisements were most skilfully worded, and might well impose upon the credulity of any one with a limited medical knowledge. My attention was first directed to Hunter's advertisements by the circumstance that one of my sisters had died of consumption, and that my mother, who was now aged, suffered remorse for not having taken her daughter to this quack. Nothing I could say seemed to relieve her morbid condition of mind. I asked a friend, an eminent physician, to have a talk with her; but he was not more successful than myself. Hunter's plausible statements were transparent enough to me, and I felt wrathful with him for the unhappiness he caused my mother. My anger with the man was increased by my knowledge of the case of a poor girl who lived in my mother's neighbourhood in the

country, and earned a scanty living as a governess. She
suffered from consumption, and had sold all her small
valuables in order to pay the fees of an ignorant pretender
who was Dr. Hunter's assistant or partner, and who had
been sent down from London to treat her. The local
practitioner, a perfectly competent man, assured me that
nothing could have been done for the poor girl, and that
the repeated visits and large fees of Hunter's assistant
were a cruel imposition.

While I was in this frame of mind Dr. Hunter was
summoned to a police-court on the charge of having
grossly insulted one of his patients. This again called
my attention to his proceedings, and I arranged with the
editor of the 'Pall Mall Gazette' for a strong article
about Hunter's practices. It happened, just at that time,
that I was making special arrangements to ensure the
paper going to press in good time. I made the manager
of the printing department responsible for the appearance of the paper at a fixed hour, and instructed him to
send a formal notice to the editors' room every afternoon,
stating the time at which the last proof *must* be returned
for press.

When the proof of the article concerning Dr. Hunter,
which was written by Mr. J. M. Capes, came down to the
editor's room, there were present, with Mr. Greenwood (the
editor) and myself, Mr. Matthew Higgins and Mr.
Fitzjames Stephen. I read the article aloud. 'Well,'
said Mr. Fitzjames Stephen, 'if you are going to print *that*
article you will hear of it!' 'At all events,' said Mr.
Higgins, 'let me take some of the worst of the libel out.'
He was a past master in that kind of work, and was
supposed to be able to write nearer libel, without actually
committing it, than any other man in London.

Higgins commenced his alterations; but before he had
gone through many lines down came the formal notice
from the manager of the printing office. We looked at

each other rather blankly; then I said, 'Hang it, let it go!' I did not quite realise what would result from my words, but I cannot say that I regret them. In the course of a few days we were served with a writ, and were in the hands of the lawyers.

We decided on a plea of justification, and had to seek our evidence. It was, of course, almost entirely medical evidence that was required, and the work of getting it together largely fell upon me. I found many of the leading doctors reluctant to appear as witnesses in a court of law, and I had a great deal of trouble in getting the evidence together. I used to spend the greater part of my mornings in the waiting-room of one doctor or another.

At length the case came on; it was tried before Lord Chief Justice Cockburn; it lasted five days and excited great interest. Nearly every newspaper in the kingdom reported it at length. My counsel were Mr. John Karslake, Q.C., Mr. Fitzjames Stephen and Mr. Quain; Mr. Coleridge, Q.C., Serjeant Parry, Mr. Hume Williams, and Mr. Cashel Hoey appeared for the plaintiff. We had a long array of distinguished doctors as witnesses: among others Dr. Charles J. B. Williams, Dr. Risdon Bennett, Dr. James Cotton, Dr. Alexander Markham, Dr. George Johnson, Dr. Quain, and Dr. William Odling, and I may offer a tribute to the generosity of the profession by stating that all my medical witnesses, with one exception, returned the fee sent to them by my solicitor. Notwithstanding this generous conduct on the part of my professional witnesses, my legal expenses were about 1,400l. The money was not entirely thrown away, for the result was a brilliant triumph for the 'Pall Mall Gazette.'

It need hardly be said that I listened to the evidence with the most anxious interest, being aware, as I was, of our weak as well as of our strong points. A doctor of great eminence in his profession had in the earlier editions

K

of an important medical work referred to the possible advantages of a treatment for consumption which by the ingenuity of counsel might be made to seem a cognate treatment to that employed by Dr. Hunter. When Mr. Coleridge took the book in his hand in the course of his cross-examination of one of our witnesses, my heart was in my boots; and when the witness left the box without any allusion having been made to the dreaded passage which might have been used with damaging effect to our cause, I involuntarily exclaimed, 'Thank God! he has missed it!' I was sitting in the reporters' box, and beside me was a gentleman, who was evidently much interested in the trial, whom I did not recognise and whom I was afraid of addressing for fear of his being a hostile witness. When I uttered the above expression he turned to me and said, 'Oh! you are on our side.' I said, 'I am the defendant;' on which he introduced himself as one of my witnesses and shook me warmly by the hand.

Dr. Williams, who was in the forefront of our phalanx of witnesses, was the medical adviser of the Lord Chief Justice, who suffered from bronchitis, and it was amusing to watch his enjoyment in questioning his own doctor, many of the questions being somewhat irrelevant to the case. The cross-examination of Dr. Hunter's two aides-de-camp, Dr. Melville and Dr. McGregor, was very severe, and one could hardly help enjoying their torture.

Among the witnesses on our side Dr. William Odling distinguished himself by the clearness and perspicuity of his exposition of abstruse scientific facts which he made quite intelligible to the jury, and under cross-examination he was a match for all Mr. Coleridge's dexterity.

Lord Chief Justice Cockburn summed up at great length. In his charge to the jury, he said the article was unquestionably marked by great severity. Language had been used of the very strongest character. But, he added, if the facts upon which the substance of the article was based were true, and it was proved that the treatment was intentionally and distinctly put forward to delude patients, and to make them Hunter's victims in purse if not in person, the libel was justifiable. 'Under such circumstances no language too strong could be employed; and to describe such a man as an impostor and a scoundrel was not an improper use of the English language.' Though Lord Chief Justice Cockburn's summing-up was marked by the usual judicial impartiality, it was soon apparent to which side his opinion tended, and with the more serious matter were introduced remarks in a lighter vein which were not calculated to give the jury a favourable impression of the plaintiff. He startled them by remarking that, according to Dr. Hunter's theory, of every four people we meet one is consumptive in either the incipient or the advanced stage; therefore three of the jury must be in that condition. But he added, in a reassuring manner, that he should have great difficulty in selecting the three, and he hoped, therefore, that the jury were an exception to the rule.

'Again,' he said, quoting Dr. Hunter, ' " if you have a hacking cough, if you have shortness of breath, if your pulse is accelerated ten or fifteen beats beyond its normal pulsation, these are infallible signs of consumption." I do not know, gentlemen, whether some of you are, like myself, getting on in the vale of years, but I do not find that I can walk up the side of a hill as I used to do. Then there is another thing; he says that "losing flesh is a sign of consumption; so is gaining flesh." You sometimes see nice rosy plump-looking young girls, the very picture of health, but he deals with them in the same way. That is nothing to the purpose: they have consumption. Especially if you change now and then, if you add to your weight at one time and lose it at another, it is consumption—consumption.'

I think if I had had no personal interest in the case I

should still have listened with the keenest pleasure to the lucid and vigorous charge of the Chief Justice, given in that musical voice for which he was famed. Fitzjames Stephen, who naturally felt a strong interest in the case, fairly beamed. He wrote on a piece of paper and passed to me the nursery rhyme :

> Take him by the right leg,
> Take him by the left leg,
> Take him by both legs
> And fling him downstairs !

The quotation was not erudite nor classical, but it adequately expressed Fitzjames Stephen's emotions. I answered him by a familiar Latin quotation, but as it is to be found in the 'Eton Latin Grammar,' I forbear to record it.

During the summing-up, Hunter, who was sitting in the well of the court, was very much excited and poured indignant comments into the ears of his counsel, until Mr. Coleridge moved away in evident disgust.

After an absence of two hours the jury returned a verdict for the plaintiff, damages one farthing. The ' damages ' were awarded, not for anything that was said about Dr. Hunter's medical practices, but for a remark upon the proceedings against him in the police court which we were not able technically to justify. This was really a most satisfactory verdict for us—for to Hunter the matter was one almost of life or death, and if he could have shown any ground for appeal we should certainly have had to fight the case over again. But, having gained his cause, he could not, of course, appeal against the verdict, and in an action for libel the jury are the sole judges of the amount of damages. When excessive damages have been given the Court of Appeal has sometimes reduced them, but I believe that in no case have the damages been increased.

On the day after the verdict there were leading articles

of a congratulatory character in most of the leading jour-
nals. The 'Times' described the action as one of equal
importance to the press and to the medical profession,
and said : ' We should fail in our duty if we did not express
our conviction that our contemporary is entitled to the
thanks of the public for a courageous attempt to protect
their interests.'

Shortly after the trial, I was presented with a very
handsome silver vase and a salver accompanied by an
address with 181 signatures which by their distinction
and authority made the address very gratifying. The
testimonial was presented ' in recognition of the important service rendered to the community by the " Pall Mall
Gazette " in successfully defending the action Hunter v.
Sharpe, whereby the freedom of the press was once more
vindicated and the right of courageous and honest criticism
affirmed.'

Public sympathy with me took other forms. I found
on my table at my office, the morning after the trial,
several envelopes, each one containing a farthing, and I
received numerous letters of congratulation, many of them
from entire strangers. On the whole, we emerged from
the action triumphantly. Hunter published a volume
defending himself, and abusing everybody on our side. I
believe that he made some attempt to bring an appeal,
but abandoned it ; in the end he left the country, and
England was afflicted with one quack the less. Hunter
was reaping a rich harvest from his dupes ; his income at
the time that the libel appeared was said to be between
12,000l. and 14,000l. a year. The trial at all events relieved me from one trouble, my anxiety about my mother.
As soon as Hunter was in a hostile position towards me,
she naturally became a keen partisan of her son : no
words were strong enough to express her indignation with
the impostor.

The next ' Pall Mall Gazette ' libel suit was one of

much literary interest.   It was brought by Mr. Hepworth
Dixon in November 1872.   Hepworth Dixon had been
announced as the chairman of the London Centenary
Festival of Sir Walter Scott.   A contributor to the ' Pall
Mall Gazette,' who was acquainted with Hepworth Dixon's
writings, wrote an ' Occasional Note' for the paper, object-
ing to the appointment to such a position of ' a man who
was best known as a writer of indecent literature.'   The
word *best* was a very unhappy superlative ; but there was
nothing for it but a plea of justification.   The difficulty
in which we were placed by the incautious use of that
word ' best ' will be easily understood ; a milder adjective
would have been quite as effective for the writer's purpose,
and justification would have been comparatively easy.
We addressed ourselves chiefly to showing what kind of
literature Mr. Hepworth Dixon had produced ; but the
only method of justifying the unhappy expression ' *best*
known ' was by attempting to show that the most indecent of Dixon's writings had had the largest sale.   We
did not make much of that contention.

It could not be expected that our counsel or solicitor
would wade through Mr. Hepworth Dixon's books, and I
had to set to work upon that unpleasant task myself, in
order to extract materials for our brief.   I got from
America pamphlets and newspapers about the various
societies of doubtful tendency which Mr. Hepworth Dixon
had described in his books—' New America' and ' Spiritual
Wives.'   It was only by connecting passages, divided by
many pages, and elucidating them by means of the
material received from America, that one could detect the
real grossness of the works.   He was a man of considerable ability, and had wrapped up his indelicacy with
great skill.

The case, which lasted three days, was tried before
Mr. Justice Brett ; the counsel for the plaintiff were
Serjeant Parry, Mr. Day, Q.C., and Mr. Gadstone ; and

we were represented by Sir John Karslake, Q.C., Mr.
Fitzjames Stephen, Q.C., and Mr. Murphy. In addition
to the 'Occasional Note' the plaintiff included in the
declaration of his cause of action an article on the work
called 'Free Russia,' which appeared in the 'Pall Mall
Gazette' more than a year previously, and which imputed
to him the publication of books which were 'obscene,
inaccurate, or both.' But of this earlier article we should
probably have heard nothing but for the appearance of
the 'Occasional Note.'

Mr. Hepworth Dixon went into the box and volun-
teered the statement that he was 'an old friend' of mine,
and that he was 'surprised at my doing him an injury.'
The 'old friendship' consisted in my having once met
him at dinner at the house of Mr. E. B. Eastwick ; and
as to my personally 'doing him an injury,' I did not see
the 'Occasional Note' until after the paper had been
printed. Sir John Karslake severely commented upon
Mr. Dixon's violation of the privileges of the press by in-
sisting on proceeding against me, as proprietor, instead of
against the publisher of the paper : but he added, as was
true, that, as it happened, I did not care about the dis-
closure of my name.

We had a consultation before going into court : Karslake told me he did not think we had any chance, and
scolded me for the 'Occasional Note' as if I had written
it myself! Once in court, however, he fought zealously
and gallantly. His speech for the defence was as fine a
piece of forensic eloquence as I have ever heard. It is
many years since, but even now I can remember the
peroration of his speech. During the trial there had been
much discussion as to the exact meaning of the word
'Mucker,' which had been used by Hepworth Dixon, and
it came generally to this, that a 'Mucker' meant a hypo-
crite and impostor. Karslake in his peroration said, 'And
this is the man who, with his pen almost wet from writing

these works, so filthy and so obscene, officiated as Chairman of the Centenary Festival of Sir Walter Scott. As
he took his place at the head of the table I can fancy the
wraith of that noble writer, who never soiled his pen
by a word that would bring a blush to the cheek of
the most innocent maiden, rising before the unworthy
Chairman, and with uplifted arm pointing at him with
his finger, and uttering the word " MUCKER " ! '

In delivering these words Karslake drew himself up to
the full height of his grand presence, and, stretching forth
his arm, pointed his finger at Hepworth Dixon with an
expression of the utmost scorn.

The verdict was for the plaintiff, with damages of
one farthing. That poor farthing was a more cruel re-
flection on Mr. Hepworth Dixon than the ' Occasional
Note ' itself.

A very amusing action for libel was that brought
against the ' Pall Mall Gazette ' by Mr. W. S. Gilbert,
the dramatist, in 1873. A letter appeared in the ' Pall
Mall Gazette,' signed ' Amuetos,' taking exception to
certain passages in a play by Mr. Gilbert then being acted
at the Haymarket Theatre, entitled ' The Wicked World.'
The criticism was not very severe in character, but Mr.
W. S. Gilbert thought fit to bring an action for libel, and
proceedings were at once instituted against us.

Mr. Gilbert also complained that the ' Pall Mall
Gazette ' had never treated him with fairness or impartiality,' and referred to many previous criticisms of his
plays.

The Judge was again Mr. Justice Brett, the counsel
for the plaintiff being the Attorney-General, Mr. J. C.
Mathew, and Mr. Montagu Williams ; and for the ' Pall
Mall Gazette ' Sir John Karslake, Q.C., and Mr. Fitzjames Stephen, Q.C.

I doubt if many more amusing cases have been tried
in a court of justice. Among the witnesses for the plain-

tiff were Mr. Buckstone, the actor, in whose part some of the criticised passages occurred, Mr. (now Sir Squire) Bancroft, and several theatrical critics.   When Mr. Buckstone went into the box there was a broad grin on the face of every one in the court.   Buckstone was a humourist of the first water; his very face was sufficient to kindle laughter; it was well-nigh impossible to look at him without smiling, and if he looked at you, you were instantly vanquished and laughed in spite of yourself.

When this well-known and inimitable visage appeared in the witness-box the court surrendered itself to mirth. Counsel, solicitors, witnesses—the very police—all grinned; and though I wish to speak with great respect of the bench, I am afraid that Mr. Justice Brett shared the universal emotion.   Karslake, in his most suave manner, invited Mr. Buckstone to repeat the lines which had been complained of.   He did so with a perfect mimicry of a schoolboy stammering through his lesson.   'No, no!' said Karslake.   'This won't do, Mr. Buckstone; we want you to repeat these lines as you do at the Haymarket Theatre.'   Buckstone fixed his eye upon the counsel, and Karslake bit his lip hard to retain his gravity.   The witness then turned to the jury, and brought his irresistible look to bear on each man in succession, and each in turn succumbed.   Then he looked at the judge, who grasped his desk with both hands and sustained Buckstone's glance, doubtless upheld by a sense of judicial responsibility.   Buckstone then turned to Karslake again, and, in a sort of stage aside, said: 'I can't, sir! I'm too *shy* !'   Every one in the court was convulsed.   The judge concealed his features by putting his face down upon his notes, but his back was eloquent.

Mr. Bancroft went into the box.   He was asked did he regard the lines criticised as immodest.   'No,' he said, in his finest manner, 'neither immodest nor indelicate.' This gave Karslake the chance of asking one of those unanswerable questions of which counsel are fond. 'Well, Mr. Bancroft,' he said, 'will you be so good as to give the jury your definition of modesty and delicacy?' The witness surveyed the counsel, the judge, the ceiling, the floor, and finally his own well-brushed hat, and he hummed and hawed, but that definition was never extracted.

The result of the trial was a verdict for the defendant.

There was one incident of this trial which, though it did not seem important at the time, one looks back upon with painful interest. It was a very dull day, and during the afternoon, while Sir John Karslake was reading with fine dramatic effect some of Gilbert's lines, candles were sent for. Sir John took one into his hands and endeavoured to continue reading, but his sight appeared to fail, and he had to hand the papers to Mr. Fitzjames Stephen. This was, I believe, the first public symptom of that illness which shortly afterwards obliged Sir John Karslake to retire from his profession, and deprived the Bar of one of its greatest ornaments and most successful advocates.

The most anxious half-hour I had in relation to a libel during my proprietorship of the 'Pall Mall Gazette' was in connection with the late Baron Grant. On arriving one morning at my office my clerk said as I went upstairs : 'There is a gentleman waiting to see you, sir, who has come from Baron Grant.' I found a tall, good-looking gentleman, in a state of great excitement. 'Are you Mr. Smith?' he demanded. I bowed. 'Are you the proprietor of the "Pall Mall Gazette"?' Another bow. 'Do you know what you have done?' 'What have I done?' Look here, sir,' he said, producing a paper ; 'do you know what has been the effect of this paragraph?' 'No,' I said. 'It has occasioned the greatest alarm among our shareholders and caused a fall in the price of our shares.' 'Well,' I asked, 'isn't the paragraph true?' 'No, sir, not a word of it!'

I examined the guilty paragraph, and it was soon apparent to me that, by an unfortunate blunder, a mere accidental slip of the pen, the Crédit Foncier, of which Baron Grant was chairman and manager, had been inserted in place of the name of another company and was described as being in liquidation. I at once saw that this was a serious matter which might involve heavy damages.

I said, 'Where is Baron Grant?' 'He is in the City trying to answer the many inquiries your paragraph has occasioned.' 'Are you going to the City?' I asked. 'Yes.' 'Then I will go with you.'

We went together and I was introduced to Baron Grant. He complained with bitterness, in which perhaps he was justified, of the paragraph. I said no one could regret the blunder more than I did; it was a pure accident, the mistake of a subordinate in the office. Anything I could do to put the matter right should be done. Baron Grant produced a handful of letters from alarmed shareholders: 'Look here, sir,' he said: 'this is what you have brought on us,' and he proceeded to pour on me much angry rhetoric. I was conscious that, in a legal sense, I was responsible, and I answered him with soft and apologetic words. My meekness seemed to make him still more violent. He began at last to talk to me as if I had committed a crime. At length I felt a little afraid of myself, and even more afraid of what might happen to Baron Grant. I stepped closer to the table, and brought my fist down upon it in a manner which made the ink-glass jump. I said, 'We have had enough of this, Mr. Gottheimer. I am not going to submit to this kind of talk any longer. I will give you the name of my solicitors, and you may communicate with them!' I was not in the humour to be amused, for I was very angry; but I think a looker-on would have found something entertaining in Baron Grant's sudden change of front; he was almost *too* apologetic. I suspect that, owing to my addressing him by his real name, he thought I knew more about him than I did, and he probably did not desire to have poured upon himself and his enterprises the harsh light of a court of law.

My one police court experience was when, on February 12, 1870, Mr. Dion Boucicault's counsel applied to Mr. Knox, the magistrate at Marlborough Street Police Court, for a summons against the publisher of the 'Pall Mall Gazette' for a libel contained in a letter signed 'Azamat-Batuk,' respecting a play called 'Formosa' which was being performed at the Princess's Theatre, a letter which he said reflected on Mr. Boucicault's private character. A summons was granted, and the parties attended at Marlborough Street on February 21. Mr. Montagu Williams, Mr. Boucicault's counsel, said that if the writer of the article would state that he did not mean to attack Mr. Boucicault's private character the avowal would be deemed satisfactory ; our counsel replied that he would readily declare on behalf of the publisher of the 'Pall Mall Gazette' that no prejudice to private character was intended. Mr. Williams demanded the name of the writer, but on the interposition of the magistrate, who pointed out that it was not usual for newspapers to disclose the names of writers and that such a demand rendered an arrangement impossible, this claim was withdrawn. The avowal was accordingly made, and the case happily came to an end.

The only libel suit in which I have been involved which has cost me more than one farthing in the way of damages was brought in June 1869 by a gentleman calling himself ' General George Henry De Strabolgie Neville Plantagenet Harrison,' who stated that he derived his title of General from one of the South American states. An article had appeared in the 'Cornhill Magazine' of April 1868 under the title of 'Don Ricardo.' It was a pleasant little gossipy article, giving an account of a visit

to Spain, describing a bull-fight, a fight between a tiger
and a bull, and between a bulldog and a donkey, with
many quaint stories told to the writer by an Englishman
resident in Madrid who was generally known as 'Don
Ricardo.' One of these stories described the amusing
adventures of a 'General Plantagenet Harrison' and his
swindling transactions. The editor of the 'Cornhill'
naturally supposed that such a name, introduced into
an article of this kind, was entirely fictitious—a mere
humorous invention of the writer. But 'General Plantagenet Harrison' presently turned up in person, in a very
angry mood, and straightway commenced an action for
libel. He had been accustomed to read for literary
purposes in the Public Record Office. This article had
drawn attention to him, and, as a result, some difficulty
had been made as to his researches at the Record Office
being allowed to continue. This constituted his claim
for damages.

I wished to insert in the next number of the 'Cornhill'
a brief explanation, with an expression of regret; but Sir
John Coleridge, our counsel (Sir John Karslake being,
unfortunately for me, unable to undertake the case), who
had seen some correspondence between the General's
solicitors and our own, in which General Plantagenet
Harrison's strange pretensions were avowed, insisted that
the whole business was a farce, and that nothing need be
done. When the General went into the witness-box his
examination and cross-examination were really very
amusing. In his evidence he admitted that he had been
in some trouble in Spain about a bill which he had left
at a bank for collection; that he had been escorted out
of Spain and imprisoned at Gibraltar; that, rightly or
wrongly, he believed himself to be descended from the
Earl of Westmoreland and the Plantagenets. His cross-
examination by the Solicitor-General, as reported in the
'Times,' revealed still more extraordinary claims.

You really believe, I understand, that you are the heir-general of Henry VI.? Yes, I do.

And that you are the rightful Duke of Lancaster, Normandy, and Aquitaine? Yes, I am.

And that your title has been recognised by the Queen under the Great Seal? Yes, in a licence to Sir F. Thesiger as Queen's Counsel to plead for me.

Her Majesty has not recognised your title in any more formal document? No.

It would be rather awkward for Her Majesty if she had, would it not? Well, I don't know.

Pray, have you asserted that you are Count of Angoulême, Flanders, Anjou, Alsace, and Champagne? Yes.

And of Kent? Yes; but that was some years ago.

In re-examination his counsel asked,

You have worked out your pedigree? Yes; I have.
And you believe it? Yes; and I can prove it.

After this evidence I thought we were safe, for I supposed that a crank of this quality must fare ill with the jury.

The writer of the article, Mr. G. H. B. Young, went into the witness-box and said that the story, or the materials for it, was told him in 1851, when he was at Madrid, by an English gentleman who was generally known as 'Don Ricardo.' The name of 'Plantagenet Harrison' was mentioned to him as that of a man travelling under that name. At that time he believed the name to be fictitious. He so believed until the plaintiff made his complaint, and down to that time he never heard of such a person as General Plantagenet Harrison, nor did he suppose at the time he wrote the article that it would apply to any living person of the name.

Mr. Justice Lush, in summing up, told the jury that even although the writer of the article was not aware of the existence of the plaintiff, yet, as he had in fact named him and had attached these imputations to his name and character, he was legally liable.

The jury returned a verdict for the plaintiff, and assessed the damages at 50*l*. I must confess the verdict took me by surprise, and I can only suppose that Sir John Coleridge's attempt to scornfully laugh the case out of court irritated the jury.

This action is a striking example of what I may call an innocent libel on the part of the writer, and I think even a publisher may claim some sympathy for the result. It is difficult to see how the editor of a periodical can protect the publisher from an action of this description. It would be clearly impossible for him to examine a writer of such an article as the one in question as to the existence of persons who were named in it; and in this particular instance it will be noticed that the writer himself believed that the name of 'Plantagenet Harrison' was fictitious.

In Memoriam

REPRINTED FROM THE 'CORNHILL MAGAZINE'
MAY 1901

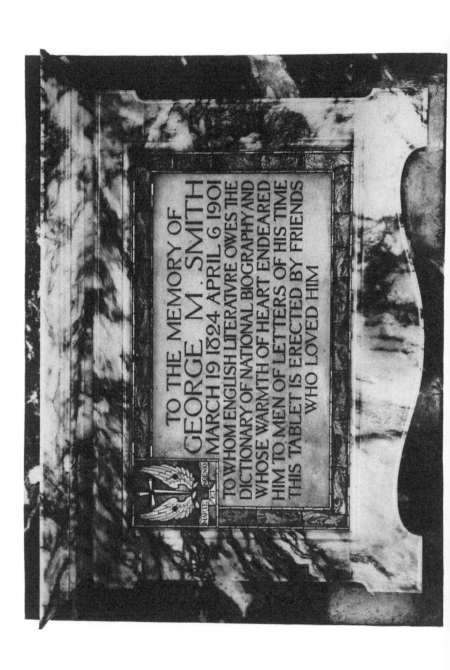

TO THE MEMORY OF
GEORGE M. SMITH
MARCH 19 1824 APRIL 6 1901
TO WHOM ENGLISH LITERATVRE OWES THE
DICTIONARY OF NATIONAL BIOGRAPHY AND
WHOSE WARMTH OF HEART ENDEARED
HIM TO MEN OF LETTERS OF HIS TIME
THIS TABLET IS ERECTED BY FRIENDS
WHO LOVED HIM

MARTE ET AGENDO

IN MEMORIAM

BUT a short time ago Mr. George Smith was interesting readers of the 'Cornhill Magazine' by drawing upon the stores of a memory familiar with our literary history for the last sixty years. Mr. Smith had known the later survivors of the first generation of the nineteenth century, and was still actively interested in literary enterprise as the century closed. He had won the cordial goodwill of innumerable authors besides publishing many of their best known works. His death (April 6, 1901) puts an end to his own narrative, which might have revealed more fully than is now possible the secret of a most honourable and in some respects unique career. Enough, however, is known to justify the strong impression made upon his contemporaries. Here I can only attempt the briefest indication of what appeared to me to be the obvious qualities to which he owed not only success in business but a most enduring hold upon the hearts of many friends.

I remember vividly my first interview with him. He was then about to start the 'Pall Mall Gazette,' and enlisted me as a contributor. I felt as I suppose a sailor must feel when he joins a ship and sees a captain beaming with cheery hopefulness and masculine self-reliance. Obviously my future captain was putting his whole heart into the enterprise, and though sanguine was cool-headed and had fully counted the cost. A good commander must, I take it, be in the first place a good man of business; and, conversely, Smith's faculty for business would have gone a

long way to the making of a leader in war. His battles
had to be fought in the law courts, not in the field; but,
as he has shown in his recent papers, he thoroughly
enjoyed such fighting as he could get. He liked the
excitement of the struggle as well as the triumph over
impostors. In early days he had shown that he possessed
the necessary combination of sagacity and daring by
taking charge of his father's business, extricating it from
difficulty, and extending its sphere of action. He was
thoroughly at home in organising and launching any new
undertaking. When, in the sixth number of the ' Cornhill
Magazine,' Thackeray boasted pleasantly of some ' late
great victories,' Smith had been the Carnot who had been
making the necessary arrangement behind the scenes.
The ' Cornhill Magazine,' and the ' Pall Mall Gazette '
after it, were new departures in their respective spheres;
and the impression made by each is a sufficient proof of the
forethought and unsparing energy which their founder
brought to bear upon those undertakings. He showed the
same spirit in many other directions. When once a business had been launched and passed into a comparatively
humdrum stage of existence, he began to thirst for some
new field of enterprise. On one side, of course, these
undertakings might be regarded simply from the financial
point of view. A man, as Johnson wisely remarks, can
seldom be employed more innocently than in making
money; and Smith, as a man of business, might claim
the benefit of that dictum. But he would not have
had positive claims upon public gratitude if he had not
combined this with loftier aims. Though he had been
immersed in business from very early youth, he took
from the first a genuine pride in his association with the
upper world of literature.

Both the ' Cornhill ' and the ' Pall Mall Gazette '
brought him into connection with the ablest writers of
the time, and provided for many of them an opportunity

of gaining a wide audience. The most conspicuous proof, however, of a disinterested love of culture was given by the Dictionary of National Biography. The first suggestion was entirely due to Smith himself; although his original plan (for a universal biographical dictionary) was too magnificent to be carried out. His part in the work was also the essential one. There would have been no difficulty in finding editors by the dozen; but if the publisher had not been ready to incur a vast expenditure, and to take for remuneration only the credit of a good piece of work, another publisher could hardly have been found to take his place. He had shown that he could be a lavishly generous publisher in his dealings with Thackeray and George Eliot. In such cases, though a mean nature does not see it, generosity may also be the best policy; but in the case of the Dictionary, the generosity was its own reward.

It was a pleasure to work with a man so much above petty considerations and so appreciative (sometimes, perhaps, beyond their merits) of men whose abilities lay in a less practical direction. The pleasure was the greater for another reason. Smith had the true chivalrous sentiment which makes thorough co-operation possible. He made me aware that he trusted me implicitly, that I could trust him equally. If anything went wrong—as things will go wrong sometimes with the most well-meaning editors—he was always ready to admit that it was the fault not of the editor but of the general perversity of things. Least of all would he ever seek to ignore his own share in any shortcoming. I sometimes thought that he carried his scrupulosity to excess. He was so anxious to show confidence and to avoid an irritating fault-finding that he would not interfere, even when a word of counsel might have done good. He was the last of men to say, ' I told you so.' A writer who had got into a serious scrape by an indiscreet publication, said to him, 'Why did you not warn me?' He would not justify himself by producing (as he could have done) a copy of the letter in which the warning had been emphatically given. That was one instance of a delicacy of feeling which was the more striking because combined with thorough straightforwardness and contempt for petty diplomacy. He could be irascible when he had to do with a knave, and could fight strenuously as well as fairly against an honourable opponent. But in all his dealings he was chivalrous to the backbone, equally incapable of striking an enemy a foul blow or of leaving a friend in the lurch.

It was not strange that such a man should win something more than sincere respect from his associates. Miss Brontë drew his portrait as he appeared to her in his early days in the Dr. John of 'Villette,' the gallant English gentleman, contemner of foppery and humbug, the ready champion of the weak, full of generous sympathy and the most sound-hearted affections. Soon afterwards he became the warm friend of Thackeray. His kindness had an opportunity in shielding an exquisitely sensitive nature from the worries of business, and between them there developed the warmest mutual regard. Thackeray would have been gratified but not surprised could it have been revealed to him that after his death his daughters would find in his old ally the most helpful and affectionate of friends and advisers. The relation to one of those daughters has continued ever since ; and she, as I well know, has valued it not only as in itself one of her best possessions, but as having been in old days a possession held in common with those who were dearest to her. Browning, whose insight was as keen as his nature was tender, became a most attached friend and spoke of their mutual confidence in his last hours. When Millais could no longer speak, he wrote that he should like to see 'George Smith, the kindest man and the best gentleman I have had to deal with.' Matthew Arnold and Smith delighted in each other, and Tom Hughes, most hearty and simple of men, found in Smith one of his most congenial friends. The men thus mentioned differed widely from each other, but all of them knew well what are the characteristics which give the best groundwork for solid and lasting friendship.

Smith impressed one first as a thorough man—masculine, unaffected, and fitted to fight his way through the world; but it was not long before one learnt to recognise the true and tender nature that went with the strength. It would be superfluous to speak of my own experience by way of confirming the judgments of which I speak. Yet I must say a word of personal gratitude. For many years I was constantly at Waterloo Place, seeing Smith and our common friend James Payn. I had had the good luck to serve as the link to bring them together; and they cordially appreciated each other. From those meetings I rarely came away without a charming—though often scandalously irrelevant—talk with one or other, and to me, as to Payn, Smith was always the gallant comrade, certain to take a bright view and to set one on better terms with oneself. I never had a word from him which left a sting; and many a fit of gloom has been dispelled by his hearty sympathy. He was a friend to be relied upon in any trouble; but, trouble or none, his sympathy was one of the permanent elements that spoke good cheer and courage in the dark moments of life. To me, as to many friends, the loss is a heavy one; the world will be to me darker and colder. I cannot even speak of those nearer to him; or I can only intimate the conviction that the necessary silence makes it impossible to do justice to his real beauty of character.

LESLIE STEPHEN.